THE
Mindfulness
Workbook
FOR
Anxiety

The 8-Week Solution to Help You Manage Anxiety, Worry & Stress

TANYA J. PETERSON, MS, NCC

ALTHEA
PRESS

For general information on our other products and services or to obtain technical support, please contact our Customer Care Department within the United States at (866) 744-2665, or outside the United States at (510) 253-0500.

Althea Press publishes its books in a variety of electronic and print formats. Some content that appears in print may not be available in electronic books, and vice versa.

Design by Thoughtfull

ISBN: Print 978-1-64152-029-4 | eBook 978-1-64152-030-0

*This workbook is dedicated to
the tens of millions of people
who experience anxiety.
This book is for you,
so you can live a mindful life,
unhindered by anxiety.*

CONTENTS

LET'S TALK ABOUT ANXIETY

Why We Struggle with Anxiety

WHAT IS ANXIETY?

Anxiety is an ogre that lives inside us and blocks us from fully living the life we want to live. Anxiety has many symptoms, both psychological and physical, that can be felt anywhere in the body. Anxiety can take hold at any time, and it can influence our thoughts, emotions, and actions.

I use *ogre* to describe anxiety because that's what it felt like to me. I lived with anxiety for most of my life. For me, it mostly showed up as an over-the-top tendency toward perfectionism, coupled with social anxiety. A therapist once described me as having an "anxious personality." Then, a traumatic brain injury, followed by two other concussions, turned my anxious tendencies into full-blown anxiety disorders. At that point, anxiety really did seem like an ogre—my own personal monster that followed me everywhere.

WHAT IS ANXIETY GOOD FOR?

To be fair, anxiety does serve a positive purpose in our lives. It can be motivating, helping us maintain peak performance. It also keeps us safe and keeps things running smoothly by ensuring we stay on the lookout for potential problems and obstacles. To a limited degree, anxiety is also a component of empathy and caring. When we love someone, we are concerned about his or her well-being, and that set of thoughts and feelings encourages us to take caring action. Anxiety becomes a problem for us when it becomes excessive. For example, when motivation becomes debilitating performance anxiety or empathy becomes overprotection and unhealthy attachment, anxiety becomes unhealthy, and we begin to struggle with it.

Fear vs. Anxiety

Fear	Anxiety
Present-focused: The source of the fear is happening now.	Past- or future-focused: The worry centers on thoughts about what already happened or what might happen.
Rational: It's a response to a threat in the outside world. Maybe your neighbor's snarling, barking dog charged at you when you walked by. Your body's fear, or fight-or-flight, reaction kicks in to help you keep yourself safe.	Irrational: Nothing directly tangible in the outside world is overtly threatening you now. You might be anxious that some snarling dog somewhere will charge at you if you go for a walk, but there isn't anything real to address.
The object of fear is real and specific.	The object of anxiety *feels* real but is vague.
Because the object of the fear is real, it's something that can be confronted. Objective measures can be taken to address it. Continuing with the snarling dog example, you can choose to take a different route, you can talk to your neighbor, or you can observe it and learn that its bark is worse than its bite.	Anxiety doesn't feel fabricated—the fear and worry you experience are real. But with anxiety, there's nothing concrete you can do to alleviate your distress, because anxiety deals in hypotheticals. Anxiety over the *possibility* of being attacked by some dog somewhere is difficult to address because the threat is theoretical.
The object of fear is external.	The object of anxiety is internal, an idea or feeling or thought. It keeps you trapped in your own mind, which can be worse than that snarling dog.

Anxiety has a close cousin—fear—that also has limited benefits and potential problems. Fear is an emotional and physiological reaction to a perceived threat. It prepares us to fight or flee, and it's designed to help us survive. Fear is a basic human instinct that, when kept in check, keeps us just vigilant enough about dangers that we take measures to protect ourselves. When a threat is real, fear is healthy. The problem is that when the brain perceives a threat that *isn't* real, the fear response is activated anyway, which can negatively impact our mood and even our physical health over time. When this happens, fear becomes an unhealthy, unhelpful cycle that keeps us on edge and prevents us from enjoying our lives.

Fear and anxiety are closely related, but the two aren't the same—even though they can *feel* the same to you when you're experiencing them. But the distinction between the two will be important to keep in mind as you work through this book. While both anxiety and fear are a combination of thoughts, feelings, and behaviors that involve worry and hypervigilance, there are key differences. The chart on page 2 offers a closer look at what those differences are.

WHEN DOES ANXIETY BECOME A PROBLEM?

People struggle with anxiety when it becomes all-encompassing, invading our thoughts and emotions, and determining our behavior. Anxiety becomes a problem when it becomes life-limiting, preventing you from living a life that reflects your goals, desires, and values.

Anxiety limits our lives by causing such uncomfortable thoughts and emotions that we begin to avoid the source of our discomfort, whether that's specific people, feelings, places, situations, or events. When you live with serious anxiety, avoidance might feel like the only thing to do that makes sense. It's a coping mechanism that feels protective and safe. If you have social anxiety and always feel judged and inadequate, you might start avoiding other people or situations where you have to interact closely with others. At first, such avoidance can actually relieve anxiety.

Eventually, however, your anxiety will find another target, and the types of things you need to avoid will grow in number. What started as a way to protect yourself from anxious feelings can actually increase those feelings. The more you hide from your anxieties, the stronger their hold over your life and your actions. Suddenly, you'll find avoidance has you trapped, and what used to be a useful coping mechanism is now a life-limiting problem.

Close your eyes for a moment and picture yourself living the life you want to live, enjoying doing fun things with people you love. Your mind is free of anxious, racing thoughts. Your emotions are mostly positive. You feel confident and balanced. Your life is yours to live.

My hope for you is that by reading this book and doing the exercises, you'll come to see that anxiety isn't who you are at your core—you don't feel anxious because you "have an anxious personality," as I was once told. You're in the grip of a set of coping strategies that have gotten out of hand and become unhealthy. With this book, you'll learn healthy mindfulness strategies to replace your anxious habits, and how to use mindfulness to gently remove yourself from anxiety's grasp. Think of mindfulness as the opposite of avoidance. Avoidance is hiding anxiously, whereas mindfulness means fully showing up for your life.

How Mindfulness Can Help

Mindfulness is an approach to mental health and well-being that involves using the senses to pay attention to what's happening around you and inside you, in the here and now. Unlike anxiety, which is focused on future possibilities and hypotheticals, mindfulness is about the present moment. Mindfulness teaches you to live in the world, while anxiety causes you to live trapped in your mind, focused on your spinning thoughts and feelings. With mindfulness, you will:

- Keep your mind occupied with what's real, leaving less room for anxious, racing thoughts and negative beliefs.

- Replace anxiety with resilience and joy.

- Take back what anxiety has stolen from you, like enjoying friendships or romantic relationships without worrying about doing something wrong. You'll be able to go to your kids' activities without being on edge, and complete a work or school assignment without dreading that it's not good enough.

WHAT IS MINDFULNESS?

People have been practicing mindfulness meditation for millennia. Ancient masters used and taught it for the same reasons we use it today—to become centered, increase well-being, and better deal with life's inevitable difficulties. The practice has been revived in our modern era, specifically as a way to deal with psychological challenges, largely through the work of Jon Kabat-Zinn. Kabat-Zinn uses his Mindfulness-Based Stress Reduction (MBSR) practice at the University of Massachusetts Medical School Stress Reduction Clinic, which he founded in 1979. News of the positive effects of mindfulness on mental and physical health has spread, and mindfulness has become increasingly popular in the United States as a result.

But what is mindfulness, exactly? Mindfulness is a type of meditation, but it's also more than meditation. Meditation, as we think of it today, is an Eastern spiritual tradition that dates back more than 5,000 years—even predating the Buddhist tradition that is often credited with starting the practice. Meditation first reached the United States in the 1960s, in a secularized form. Meditation is a broad term for the practice of turning inward and becoming still. It includes mindfulness, yoga, and more. Mindfulness includes this, and is also bigger than this. Mindfulness is a way of being with yourself and perceiving the world around you that can help you live your life more peacefully and with greater equanimity. Jon Kabat-Zinn, due to his work at the University of Massachusetts Medical School, is regarded by many as the founder of the modern mindfulness movement.

HOW MINDFULNESS TECHNIQUES HELP WITH ANXIETY

For our purposes here, the most important thing to remember about mindfulness is that it *works*. Be confident in the fact that research supports the effectiveness of mindfulness for reducing anxiety. For example, University of California, Los Angeles researchers reviewed a number of studies and found that mindfulness benefits the brain by protecting us from stress and enhancing our decision-making techniques. In a 2011 study reported in *Psychiatry Research: Neuroimaging*, researchers discovered that practicing mindfulness changes the brain in positive ways, such as increasing gray matter (areas of the brain containing nerve cell bodies). One of the many areas comprised of gray matter is the hippocampus, a structure involved in learning, memory, emotional control, and stress arousal and responsiveness. The hippocampus is one of the parts of the brain responsible for anxiety. Through mindfulness, the study's researchers report, we can increase the gray matter in the hippocampus, effectively strengthening it and helping it better withstand stress, and thereby reduce anxiety.

So, we've established that mindfulness definitely works to reduce anxiety, so you can reclaim your life and live fully and freely. However, its strategies can be challenging to learn, and they can take some getting used to. Anxiety is used to having a lot of control over your brain, and it won't give up its power easily. You might experience frustration and doubt along the way. *Am I doing this right? Why do I still feel anxious? Why is it that no matter what I do, my mind won't stay focused and goes right back to ruminating and fretting?* These are common questions and challenges people face when learning to decrease anxiety through mindfulness practices. Know that these thoughts, and others like them, are normal and par for the course. Learning to implement mindfulness is a process, more than a quick fix—though you will likely feel some subtle changes right away. Still, there are ways to shift your thinking about this process that will help make your mindfulness journey more enjoyable and less frustrating.

Let these mental skills gently guide you as you progress through this workbook. They're based, in part, on principles taught by mindfulness expert Jon Kabat-Zinn, so they fit right into our program.

- **Nonjudgment.** Anxious thoughts involve rules, absolutes, and "shoulds." Instead of berating yourself for perceived shortcomings, approach the present moment without judging it.

- **Patience.** Be kind to yourself as you develop a mindful lifestyle, knowing that it's a process with a lot of stops and starts.

- **Beginner's mind:** Approach your anxious thoughts with the mind-set of a beginner, someone who doesn't have all the answers. That way, when anxiety tries to convince you of something, you are open to the fact that there are other possibilities.

Using mindfulness for anxiety will become a way of life. This book will guide you along your path to peace of mind.

HOW TO USE
THIS BOOK

How to Use This Book

You are about to learn how to take back your mind, and your life, from anxiety. The mindfulness exercises and anxiety strategies you'll be using are evidence-based—they've been proven to work. Mindfulness is one of the most powerful and effective ways to replace anxiety with peace, calm, and happiness, while the exercises based on psychotherapy techniques have decades' worth of studies showing their effectiveness in reducing anxiety symptoms.

The program outlined in this book will guide you through both mindfulness skills exercises and anxiety-focused exercises—the latter of which were developed by psychologists and other anxiety experts. The two types of strategies will alternate weekly: one week will focus on building tools for your mindfulness skill set and the next week will focus on exercises that target different types or aspects of anxiety. Both of these types of skills are interrelated and closely connected to each other. Learning about your anxiety and doing exercises designed to target it will help you experience fewer of the symptoms that are causing you problems—worry, anxiety, and avoidance. At the same time, learning mindfulness skills will help you create more of what you *do* want—inner peace, calm, and the ability to enjoy life. All of the exercises reinforce and support each other to provide you with a strong base from which to grow.

WORKING THE EIGHT-WEEK PROGRAM

The book is designed as an eight-week path to a mindful life with less anxiety. Each of the eight weeks has an activity or exercise designed to build and strengthen the skills that will help you manage and decrease your anxiety symptoms. Every week you'll be presented with three main exercises, designed to be done twice each, back-to-back. Those exercises will take you through the first six days of your week.

The exercises will vary in nature. Some will be quiet meditations, others will be writing exercises, and some will involve you taking some sort of action. You'll also be given homework at the end of each week to round things off and reflect on what you've learned.

To get the full benefit of this program, it's important to do all of the exercises and homework in the order they're presented. The exercises will teach you skills you need to take charge of your anxiety symptoms and make real change. After all, you'll need to act differently if you want to start getting different results. The exercises and meditations are designed to be gradual, guided steps toward living differently. When you use this book intentionally, doing all of the exercises and applying them in your daily life, you can expect to build a collection of strategies and skills to help you live more fully in each moment of your life, with more mindfulness and less anxiety.

That said, this is your book. You can take the exercises and readings at your own pace, if doing the full eight weeks at once is more than you can manage with your schedule. Remember that one of the mental skills of mindfulness is nonjudgment. Don't worry about how you do the program or judge the way you're approaching the book and exercises. Take the book day by day, and skill by skill, and know that you are doing it the right way for you.

Finally, some of the exercises in the mindfulness chapters take the form of short meditations. These exercises include a time that you're recommended to do them—you'll see "5 minutes" or "10 minutes," etc., written at the top of the exercise. Please be aware that you can always do these meditations for longer than the recommended time if you're enjoying them and it fits into your schedule.

Before You Get Started

Sticking to the eight-week schedule is the best way to see immediate results. However, life happens, and it's not the end of the world if you have to skip a day here and there, just so long as you pick up where you left off. To maximize your chances of staying on track, plan to set aside time each day to read and complete the exercises. Perhaps begin with 15 or 20 minutes per day, and adjust that as needed. Make each exercise special with a cup of tea or coffee, or some other small treat you enjoy.

It's a good idea to have a notebook to use along with the workbook. There are times you'll want to write more than space on the workbook pages allows, and there will also be homework assignments and journaling prompts to deepen the experience for you. You'll see this icon when you need your notebook:

Now, you're ready for the journey into the present moment, so let's begin.

PRESENT MOMENT AWARENESS

WEEK 1

YOUR WEEK

You'll find a schedule like this one at the beginning of each new week. Think of it as a suggested guideline rather than a rigid timeline. You can read the text and do the exercises as many times as you wish.

Here's your first weekly schedule:

DAY 1

READ:
The Challenge and The Solution

EXERCISE:
Breath Awareness Meditation
(5 minutes)

DAY 2

EXERCISE:
Breath Awareness Meditation
(10 minutes)

EXERCISE:
Breath Awareness in the
Waiting Place

DAY 3

EXERCISE:
Mindfully Eat an Orange
(10 minutes)

DAY 4

EXERCISE:
Experience a Bowl of Cereal
(15 minutes)

EXERCISE:
Recipe for Reduced Anxiety

DAY 5

EXERCISE:
Open Awareness (10 minutes)

DAY 6

EXERCISE:
Open Awareness (15 minutes)

EXERCISE:
Open Awareness of Yourself and
the Moment

DAY 7

HOMEWORK

DAY 1

The Challenge

Sometimes our thoughts can work against us. Thinking is at the heart of anxiety, and when our worries put our minds on autopilot or we get carried away thinking about future plans, we're effectively abandoning the present moment to live in our thoughts.

However, the act of thinking itself isn't a problem. Thinking is extremely useful! It's thinking that allows us to navigate the days of our lives and all of the complex things we deal with, like other people and rapidly changing situations. Thinking allows us to plan and to make the thousands of decisions, ranging from tiny to huge, that we have to make every day. Thinking enables us to process what's happening and respond in appropriate ways—it's essential to our lives.

The problems arise when we let our thoughts take over. When we give them too much power, they can make us unhappy even when life is going well, and we can miss out on what's going on around us and start living in the world our thoughts build. You can tell thinking has become a problem when:

- Thoughts race away and take your focus and attention with them.

- The brain becomes hypervigilant, constantly thinking about potential problems; what we look for, we tend to find.

- You become trapped in anxious thoughts and miss out on the real world and the good things in it—your actual life, not your thoughts about it.

Are there times in your own life when overthinking has created problems with anxiety and stress? Maybe you've experienced something similar to these situations:

- You had to give a presentation, and you were so worried about people judging you that you kept losing track of where you were in the presentation.

- You felt so extremely anxious being in a crowded store that all you could think about was needing to get out. Your thoughts raced with concern about your pounding heart, difficulty breathing, problematic vision, and your panic increased. A simple shopping trip became an ordeal.

So often in scenarios like these, our thoughts are the biggest challenge we face. No matter how much you hate giving presentations or being in crowded stores, those situations aren't the real problem. The truth is, you can handle these stressful situations because they're temporary, and you're strong and resilient and have lots of coping strategies. But if you listen to what your anxious thoughts tell you about those situations—that they're terrible and must be avoided at all costs—you can (unintentionally) make everything worse.

Mindfulness can help with the problems of overthinking, because it teaches us to redirect our thoughts and focus our attention with intention and purpose. We attend to what's around us instead of to anxious thinking, we refocus and consciously *choose* what we pay attention to.

The Solution: Present Moment Awareness

The solution to overthinking and anxiety's racing thoughts is to focus your attention on the present moment. Instead of struggling with your anxious thoughts, embrace the moment you're in. Perhaps surprisingly, with present moment awareness you won't be trying to stop your thoughts or argue with them. While resisting anxiety might seem like the obvious solution, as it turns out, that never really works.

If you've ever tried to get a small child to stop having a tantrum by telling him to "stop it," or by arguing with him, you know that struggling like this only intensifies the behavior you're trying to stop. Our thoughts—particularly the anxious ones—can be like toddlers having tantrums. The more we fight with them, the louder and more persistent they become.

Instead, training yourself to be mindfully aware of what is happing right now, in this moment, shifts your focus. The anxious thoughts are still there, you're just paying less attention to them. Like the toddler, attention is what these thoughts *want*, and when you deprive them of it they gradually lose strength. As you hone the skill of focused awareness, you become more conscious of yourself and your surroundings. Awareness balances thinking and reduces anxiety, because while anxiety is focused on the past or the future, awareness is grounded in the present.

To practice present moment awareness, you pay attention, on purpose, to the present with as many of your senses as is practical in that moment. Our thoughts can get in the way of our ability to experience life in all its sensory complexity, but intentionally showing up for *this* moment and all the sounds and sights and smells that come with it, helps start to crowd out your anxious thoughts with more centered ones.

Awareness is a tool that you can use to tame your thoughts, reduce anxiety, and focus fully on what you're doing in the here and now. In doing so, you'll cultivate your sense of peace, equanimity, and joy—things that are much more pleasant and fun than feeling anxious about what has happened in the past, or what may happen in the future.

One last quick note before we dive into the exercises: You will have the opportunity to learn and practice many different mindfulness activities as you read this book. A few important guidelines will help you benefit from them fully.

- Incorporate the principles of nonjudgment, patience, and beginner's mind.

- There's no such thing as right or wrong when you do these exercises. Mindfulness is not the absence of anxiety or racing thoughts. It's the process of pulling our minds back from these and into the present moment.

- The point is not to try to vanquish anxiety or force a new way of thinking. Instead, you're gently adding a new way of being that will, by default, reduce anxiety.

- Simply be—allow things just to be as they are, including yourself.

EIGHT THINGS MINDFULNESS IS NOT

There are a lot of misunderstandings about mindfulness. This list of eight common mindfulness misconceptions should clarify what mindfulness is *not*. This, in turn, will help you understand what mindfulness really *is* and how it can help you reduce anxiety and live the life you want.

Mindfulness is not:

A QUICK-FIX TRICK: The biggest benefits of mindfulness happen as you keep practicing it over time.

RELIGIOUS: Mindfulness isn't part of a religion, and it doesn't involve beliefs or practices that conflict with any religion.

SOMETHING SEPARATE FROM YOU: The capacity to be mindful comes from within.

TIME-LIMITED: It's not something that you only do for eight weeks and then put on a shelf, because the more you practice mindfulness, the better it works.

SOMETHING YOU HAVE TO "DROP EVERYTHING" FOR: Mindfulness is a mind-set and way of life that fits in with where you are and what you're doing.

A MAGIC WAND OR CURE-ALL: It's a tool—a very effective one—that you can use to choose your focus, reduce anxiety, and still face problems but live a quality life.

JUST FOR PEOPLE WHO ARE ALREADY RELAXED AND FULL OF INNER PEACE: Mindfulness is a powerful way of taking charge of your anxiety and becoming relaxed and full of inner peace.

ALWAYS EASY: You do have the natural ability to live mindfully, but doing so takes patience and practice. You can learn mindfulness and reap the many mental health benefits. Just know that it's a skill that must be developed, and don't give up!

Breath Awareness

Deep, belly breathing has an instant calming effect on the brain and lowers your blood pressure and heart rate. Breath awareness is a tool that you can use discreetly anywhere, anytime, to reduce anxiety.

EXERCISE

BREATH AWARENESS MEDITATION (5 MINUTES)

1. Get comfortable by sitting or lying down.

2. Set your timer for 5 minutes.

3. You can choose to keep your eyes opened or closed. Raise your arms above your head and then clasp your hands behind your head.

4. Breathe in slowly, through your nose. Hear the air moving into your body. Feel it in your nose, your throat. Watch your belly expand.

5. Pause briefly and feel your body hold the air.

6. Exhale slowly through your mouth, feeling the air pass across your lips as your belly relaxes.

7. When your thoughts wander, simply return them to the sound and feel of the air entering and exiting your body.

8. Repeat for the duration of the meditation. You can use breath awareness to ground yourself at any point in your day. If you're in a long line, stuck in traffic, or anxious about meeting a group of people, take a minute or two to tune in to your breath. Do this as many times as you can throughout the day.

DAY 2

BREATH AWARENESS MEDITATION (10 MINUTES)

Today, you'll repeat yesterday's exercise, this time sitting in breath awareness a little longer.

1. Get comfortable by sitting or lying down.

2. Set your timer for 10 minutes.

3. You can choose to keep your eyes opened or closed. Raise your arms above your head and then clasp your hands behind your head.

4. Breathe in slowly, through your nose. Hear the air moving into your body. Feel it in your nose, your throat. Watch your belly expand.

5. Pause briefly and feel your body hold the air.

6. Exhale slowly through your mouth, feeling the air pass across your lips as your belly relaxes.

7. When your thoughts wander, simply return them to the sound and feel of the air entering and exiting your body.

8. Repeat for the duration. You can use breath awareness to ground yourself at any point in your day. If you're in a long line, stuck in traffic, or anxious about meeting a group of people, take a minute or two to tune in to your breath. Do this as many times as you can throughout the day.

BREATH AWARENESS IN THE WAITING PLACE

Anxiety often spikes when we have to wait—in line, at a red light, for the bus, in an office waiting room. for a slow webpage to load, for water to boil. Waiting times are breeding grounds for anxiety because, without a focus, our thoughts run wild.

Ah, but you do have a focus! It's present moment awareness in which you pay purposeful attention to your breathing.

1. List seven examples (one for each day of the week) where you likely find yourself waiting.

_____

_____

_____

_____

_____

_____

_____

2. During these times, practice breath awareness.

3. Reflect on how your body and mind respond. Breath awareness didn't change the fact that you were stuck at a red light, of course, but how did it make a difference in your inner experience?

_____

_____

_____

_____

_____

_____

Mindful Eating

Mindful eating allows you to use all of your senses, even taste, to practice mindful awareness of the present moment. You can eat mindfully whether it's a small snack or a full meal. The idea is to pay attention with all your senses to what you are doing—in this case, eating—right now.

EXERCISE
MINDFULLY EAT AN ORANGE (10 MINUTES)

1. Set your timer for 10 minutes. Make sure the immediate environment is distraction-free. Put away your cell phone and turn off the television.

2. Hold an orange in your hands, gently cupping it to feel its round shape and experience its weight.

3. Rub your fingertips along the peel and observe the subtle, rubbery texture.

4. Pierce it with your fingernail to open it. Feel the juice run onto your finger.

5. Lift it to your nose, watching the orange come close, and breathe in deeply, reveling in the scent.

6. Put your tongue on the exposed part of the fruit and let a bit of juice settle on your tongue. Note the feel of the liquid and the taste of the juice.

7. Now, peel it completely. Rub the peel between your fingertips and note the contrast between the outside and inside. Feel the stickiness of the juice.

8. Listen to the sound the orange makes as you gently separate the segments.

9. Visually explore the nuances of color, the textured lines, and the small white seeds.

10. Eat the orange slowly, taking small bites out of each segment and chewing and swallowing deliberately. How does it feel in your hands? Your mouth? How does it taste?

EXPERIENCE A BOWL OF CEREAL (15 MINUTES)

1. Set your timer for 15 minutes. Make sure the immediate environment is distraction-free. Put away your cell phone and turn off the television or radio.

2. Select your bowl and spoon. Feel the empty bowl in your hands and note if it is completely smooth or if it has texture, ridges, etc. Feel the spoon. Close your eyes and run your fingers over it, feeling the edges, the concave and convex sides.

3. Pour cereal into the bowl. Listen to the sound the pieces make as they land in the bowl. Stir them a bit with your spoon and watch them move.

4. Watch the milk as you pour it over the cereal. Is it a tiny trickle or more of a flow? Notice it work its way around, though, and under the cereal. Push your spoon down on the cereal. What does it do in the milk?

5. Put your ear to the bowl. Does your cereal make any sounds?

6. Dip your spoon into the bowl, fill it with cereal, and slowly raise the spoon to your mouth. Take a bite. What do the cereal, milk, and spoon feel like in your mouth? Note the temperature as well as the contrast between liquid and solid.

7. Begin to chew slowly. Feel the crunch with your teeth. Listen to the sound the cereal makes as you chew it. Notice the taste.

8. Continue to eat slowly and mindfully, paying attention to the cereal and your act of eating it.

RECIPE FOR REDUCED ANXIETY

In this exercise, you will plan your own mindful eating experience. This is one of the first steps you'll take toward integrating mindfulness into your daily life.

1. Choose a favorite recipe. Write down why it's your favorite. What about it makes you happy?

_____

_____

_____

_____

2. Prepare it mindfully. This means paying purposeful attention to each step with all of your senses. Reflect and contemplate what it's like to pay such close attention to what you are doing rather than having your mind race.

_____

_____

_____

_____

_____

3. When it is ready, enjoy it by eating mindfully the way you did with the orange and the cereal. Reflect on how this experience is different from how you normally eat meals. List two or three ways this experience made a positive difference for you.

_____

_____

_____

_____

_____

Open Awareness

With open awareness, you'll let your senses wander and tune in to whatever passes through your consciousness, whether it's a sound, a smell, or a physical sensation. Open awareness isn't the same as having a wandering mind, because when the mind wanders it often strolls over to anxiety's neighborhood. Open awareness is the mindful noticing of all sensory input without deciding to focus on one thing over the other, which helps maintain mental equilibrium. We just notice things as they float in and out of our awareness, without judging or responding to them.

EXERCISE

OPEN AWARENESS (10 MINUTES)

1. Find a location where you'll feel comfortable. Outdoors is ideal, but if that's not possible, indoors is just fine.

2. Set your timer for 10 minutes.

3. Notice the sights, sounds, smells, and textures of things you can feel with your hands—the chair, the fabric of your pants.

4. Let the sensory input come and go. If you notice something with your eyes, pay attention to it. When a sound takes over, listen to it.

5. When your thoughts turn to anxieties, tune back in to any of your senses and redirect your focus to what you see, hear, smell, or feel.

6. Continue for the duration.

DAY 6

EXERCISE

OPEN AWARENESS (15 MINUTES)

Today, you'll engage again in this open awareness meditation. This time, you'll challenge yourself by staying with it a bit longer.

1. Find a comfortable position. Outdoors is ideal, but if that's not possible, indoors is just fine.

2. Set your timer for 15 minutes.

3. Notice the sights, sounds, smells, and textures of things you can feel with your hands—the chair, the fabric of your pants.

4. Let the sensory input come and go. If you notice something with your eyes, pay attention to it. When a sound takes over, listen to it.

5. When your thoughts turn to anxieties, tune back in to any of your senses and redirect your focus to what you see, hear, smell, or feel.

6. Continue for the duration.

EXERCISE

OPEN AWARENESS OF YOURSELF AND THE MOMENT

 This exercise will help develop awareness of what's going on within you and around you. It will guide your focus to stay in the present moment.

1. Jot down what's going on inside your brain and body. What thoughts are you experiencing? Emotions? Physical sensations?

2. Now, turn your awareness to what's around you. In an open awareness style, write down what you notice with your senses.

3. Without pausing, begin to write down what's going on in your brain and body.

4. What changed when you shifted your focus?

5. How and where can you best use open awareness in your life? List some places or situations when this might be a useful skill to use.

Homework

Your notebook will become a close companion as you progress through this book. Through each exercise, you'll acquire the skills to help you become more mindful and present, and to live your life without being bullied by anxiety. These new skills will eventually evolve into habits, and soon you'll develop the confidence to be fully and mindfully present in life.

Make this reflection time special. Make a cup of coffee, tea, or hot chocolate (and sip mindfully); grab your favorite pen; and sit in a quiet, comfortable place. Reflect on these questions:

1. What were your biggest challenges in being mindful in the present moment?

2. What made you keep going despite these obstacles?

3. Were there times and/or places that were easier to be present in than others?

4. If so, what was different?

5. In what situations will practicing present moment awareness be especially helpful to you?

TAKEAWAYS

- Mindfulness is living in your present moment rather than in your anxious thoughts and feelings.

- The mental skills of nonjudgment, patience, and beginner's mind will guide you as you learn to practice mindfulness to reduce anxiety.

- Our thoughts about certain situations, rather than the situations themselves, lead to anxiety.

- The solution to overthinking and to the racing thoughts of anxiety is present moment awareness.

WORRY & RUMINATION

YOUR WEEK

DAY 1

READ:
The Challenge and The Solution

COMPLETE:
Anxiety Checklist

EXERCISE:
Separating What is Possible from
What is Probable (Part One)

DAY 2

EXERCISE:
Separating What is Possible from
What is Probable (Part Two)

EXERCISE:
What Will Replace Your Anxiety?

DAY 3

EXERCISE:
What Are Your Worry Triggers?
(Part One)

DAY 4

EXERCISE:
What are Your Worry Triggers?
(Part Two)

EXERCISE:
Recording Recurrent Worries

DAY 5

EXERCISE:
Who's Driving Your Worry Car?

DAY 6

EXERCISE:
The Downward Arrow

DAY 7

HOMEWORK

The Challenge

Everybody worries. Often we blame ourselves for worrying so much, being anxious, or being too stressed out. But now it's time to lay that guilt and self-blame to rest, because worrying is one of the things our brains naturally *do*, just like our lungs naturally breathe and our hearts beat. We come into this world observing and assessing our surroundings to make sure we're safe. Worry that is focused on a specific situation can be helpful to us. It can help us anticipate problems and prevent bad outcomes. When worry is focused on an external issue that needs solving, it's usually not a problem.

But chronic worrying can lead to anxiety and trap the mind in a cycle with no resolution. Worry and anxiety often go hand in hand, but they aren't the same thing. Anxiety is an all-encompassing experience that can affect our thoughts, feelings, behaviors, and physical health. Worry is a mostly word-based *manifestation* of anxiety. It is a symptom of anxiety that is verbally generated, as opposed to showing up as a physiological symptom (racing heart, shortness of breath) or as emotion (anger, despair). Worries are a chain of thoughts, and thoughts are verbal: *What will happen if . . . ? It will be terrible when . . . What if I can't . . . ?* Worry is based in words. It is the fearful thinking that feeds off of our anxiety and causes us to imagine and dwell on worst-case scenarios: *What if my PowerPoint doesn't work? What if my boss thinks I'm an idiot? What if I'm fired?* This kind of worry cycle is known as *rumination*.

Let's look at one woman's experience of suffering from rumination:

Diane is a wife and a mother of two children. One weekend, her husband, Phil, suggested a family hike. Because she had a long to-do list, she opted to stay home. Not 10 minutes after Phil and the kids left, she regretted her decision to stay home. She began to worry about all the things that could go wrong in her absence. *What if the kids act up and Phil can't handle them by himself? What if they run off and get lost? What if someone gets hurt? What if something happens to Phil and he can't drive? How will they get back home? I should have gone along.*

Diane's worry was taking up so much of her energy that she found she wasn't getting to any of the items on her to-do list—and she started worrying about that, too. *I'm not getting my work done anyway. What if I don't get it done by Monday and I get fired? How will we get by on just one income? What if that isn't an issue because Phil and the kids don't come back? What if something happens and they die? And I've been so irritable lately. What if they're alive but just don't want to come back?* Diane's thoughts raced with worry, one anxious thought leading to the next, until she actually felt sick. The pressure in her head wasn't even relieved by the tears that began to fall.

Rumination, or repeatedly returning to the same anxious thoughts, keeps reminding you of your worries, so the perceived problems are constantly on your mind and seem to grow bigger each time you revisit them. Worry and rumination can be about anything and everything: health, happiness, family, relationships, work, finances. You name it, and you can probably find a way to worry about it. Many people report that it seems like there's no end to their worries. That's because once worries start to run amok, there's often nothing concrete we can *do* to address them. Diane's worries ran away with her

YOU'RE NOT A COW

You might remember from high school biology that cows chew their cud. Sheep, goats, camels, antelope, deer, and giraffes are among the many others that do it, too. These animals have four stomachs, and to digest their food they regurgitate it and chew it again. They can't let the food move on after they swallow it the first time but instead need to bring it back up and work it some more.

Animals that regurgitate and chew the cud are called *ruminants*. In a way, humans are ruminants, too. Four-stomached animals chew and chew and chew on their food. We humans endlessly chew over our thoughts. We *ruminate* on them, going over them in our minds repeatedly.

Cows have to ruminate. It's just how their digestive system works, and nothing they do will change it. But you're not a cow! You don't have to ruminate to process your thoughts, spinning your thoughts around in your mind and returning to them in an endless loop. Unlike a cow, you have the power of choice, and the advanced ability to stop ruminating and start living with a constant supply of fresh thoughts, many of which come by living mindfully in each moment.

until she thought that her family wouldn't come home from hiking. The worry was imagined, so there was no action she could take to address it. Instead, she ruminated and her worries grew more intense and overwhelming.

When there's something concrete you can do to resolve worry, such as rattle a doorknob to make sure it's locked, it's easier to move past it. It's rooted in something real that can be seen, heard, or felt.

In contrast, anxiety and excessive worry are often irrational and have no concrete solution, so they can take over your thinking and even your life—there's nothing concrete you can do about them, and there's no end in sight.

Ah, but there *is* a way out! Let's take a look at the pathway out of worry and ruminative thoughts.

The Solution: Recognizing Irrational Thinking

It's important to understand that irrational thinking often dominates our worries and anxiety. Irrational thinking causes us to believe that there are no corresponding solutions to our problems, and nothing can be done to prevent the bad outcomes—it's just going to be *bad*.

But just because you think something is true, and you're able to tell a convincing story about why it's true, *does not mean it actually is true*. This is a hard lesson for most of us to learn, because our thoughts are very convincing and, in most cases, they steer us in the right direction. But our anxious thoughts can also easily steer us wrong.

Each and every one of us, whether we realize it or not, develops theories about how things work. We formulate ideas about ourselves, others, and the world in general, and we use these theories to predict what is likely to happen to us and plan accordingly.

But we also have beliefs that are driven by anxiety and worry—which means they're less rational and also less helpful. You'll be exploring and addressing them in the exercises in this chapter. It's useful to first know the general nature of some of your theories. Do you recognize your own beliefs among these examples? Put a ✓ by any that resonate with you. Add others that come to mind.

Anxiety Checklist

- [ ] People can't be trusted.
- [ ] The world is unsafe.
- [ ] If I stop worrying, bad things will happen. Therefore, I must worry.
- [ ] If I don't worry, it means that I don't care enough.
- [ ] People don't mean what they say, so I can't believe praise and compliments.
- [ ] I'm not good enough to _____.
- [ ] Problems only get worse.
- [ ] If something is wrong, then nothing is okay.
- [ ] So many things can go wrong with my body to make me unhealthy.
- [ ] The world is full of unhealthy things, and it only makes sense to worry about the effects.
- [ ] I am powerless to change anything, so all I can do is worry.
- [ ] If I make mistakes, consequences are always bad.
- [ ] At any moment, my partner or friends will leave me.
- [ ] Things could get so bad that I won't be able to handle them.
- [ ] Worrying is what protects me.
- [ ] If I get criticized for something, it means everything I do is bad.
- [ ] I tend to drive people away, but I don't mean to.
- [ ] Nothing can be counted on to stay the same.
- [ ] The economy isn't stable, and I could lose everything at any time.
- [ ] "Worried sick" is the only state I feel comfortable being in, even though I hate it.
- [ ] _____
- [ ] _____
- [ ] _____

The exercises that follow are designed to help you examine your thoughts more closely and loosen the hold they have on you.

Worst-Case Scenarios

No matter which theories are driving your anxiety, the result is that your worries get blown out of proportion until they feel too big to handle. This is known as "catastrophizing," or believing that everything is or will be a disaster. In Diane's example, you saw how normal concern about safety escalated until her husband was injured and her kids were unable to return home to safety.

One way to help you learn to bring your catastrophic thoughts back down to size is to reframe them as outcomes that are *possible*, but not *probable*. Thinking in terms of probability is a great place to start shrinking anxiety down to its proper size. Let's look at the differences between *possible* and *probable* outcomes:

Possible (Irrational)	Probable (Rational)
The kids will run off and get lost.	The kids will be full of energy and will run ahead, but her husband, an adult, can handle them.
Your soccer-playing daughter will break her arm during the game.	If she does get hurt, which she might not, a broken arm isn't a common soccer injury. Most injuries won't disrupt school or music.
Aaron's enormous credit card debt will leave him homeless.	Aaron will have to restructure his finances, change his spending habits, and slowly pay off his debt, but he won't lose his home.

SEPARATING WHAT IS POSSIBLE FROM WHAT IS PROBABLE (PART ONE)

Now think of your own anxieties and worries. In the left column, write down what your anxiety is telling you is *possible*. Then, refocus and in the right column, write what outcome is *probable* and more realistic. Begin with just three or four worries.

Possible (Irrational)	Probable (Rational)

EXERCISE

SEPARATING WHAT IS POSSIBLE FROM WHAT IS PROBABLE (PART TWO)

Add additional worries and what seems *possible* according to your anxiety and what seems *probable*, or more likely.

Possible (Irrational)	Probable (Rational)

WHAT WILL REPLACE YOUR ANXIETY?

As you continue to identify your worries and label which ones are *possible* and which are *probable*, how will things improve for you? Go deeper than "my anxiety will lessen." What positive things will begin to take the place of anxiety and worry? In other words, *why* do you want to keep doing this exercise beyond this workbook? (Note: This is a helpful way to reflect on all of the exercises and information you're learning here!)

Worry Triggers

We have issues that we worry about, and there is a wide spectrum of things that trigger those worries. Sometimes we're not aware of why we're worrying, when we're doing it, or what we tend to worry about the most. We just know that we feel anxious. We know that we're ruminating. We know that we are stuck in a cycle of worry and that we want out.

One of the ways to break the cycle of worry is to be aware of which things trigger our anxiety. Is it when we're in certain places? Particular times of the day? Specific people? Many different things can trigger worry, and understanding your particular triggers can help you process and establish ways to respond to your anxious feelings.

EXERCISE
WHAT ARE YOUR WORRY TRIGGERS? (PART ONE)

By identifying those triggers and shifting your thinking, you can stop your worrying before it starts. This exercise will help increase your awareness of your worry triggers.

1. Pick one worry from the chart you completed on page 33 and write it down here.

_____

_____

2. When do you find yourself worrying about this?

_____

_____

3. Where are you when this worry is at its peak?

_____

_____

_____

4. How is your physical state (nutrition, hydration, sleep, exercise, etc.)?

_____

_____

_____

_____

5. What makes it worse?

_____

_____

_____

_____

6. What makes it better?

_____

_____

_____

_____

7. Now, look back at your chart again. Do you notice any themes to your worry? What are they? For example, you might notice that many of your worries are about relationships. Or perhaps you worry a lot about your role as a parent, employee, boss, etc. Or maybe you worry about lots of different things. List your prominent worry theme(s).

_____

_____

_____

_____

_____

DAY 4

WHAT ARE YOUR WORRY TRIGGERS? (PART TWO)

Continue exploring what triggers your worry by repeating yesterday's exercise, this time using a different worry.

1. Pick one worry from the chart you completed on page 33 and write it down here.

_____

_____

2. When do you find yourself worrying about this?

_____

_____

_____

_____

3. Where are you when this worry is at its peak?

_____

_____

_____

_____

4. How is your physical state (nutrition, hydration, sleep, exercise, etc.)?

_____

_____

_____

_____

5. What makes it worse?

_____

_____

_____

_____

6. What makes it better?

_____

_____

_____

_____

7. Now, look back at your chart again. Do you notice any themes to the worry? What are they? For example, you might notice that many of your worries are about relationships. Or perhaps you worry a lot about your role as a parent, employee, boss, etc. Or maybe you worry about lots of different things. List your prominent worry theme(s).

_____

_____

_____

_____

_____

EXERCISE

RECORDING RECURRENT WORRIES

Keep a running journal entry to record worry patterns and themes. Think of the exercise you just did. What do you notice about your anxiety? What changes can you make in your worry triggers in order to reduce anxiety?

Your Worry Car

When we clearly see the underlying beliefs—our theories about how things work—that drive our anxieties, we can revise them in a healthier, more rational way.

EXERCISE

WHO'S DRIVING YOUR WORRY CAR?

1. Look back at the list of theories behind your worries on page 31. Note the ones you checked, and write them down here. These are some of the beliefs that drive your worry car.

_____

_____

_____

_____

2. Next, for each belief you listed, rate how realistic it is on a scale from 1 to 10, with 1 being not at all realistic, and 10 signifying that it could actually happen.

_____

_____

_____

_____

3. It's also helpful to question what started the worry car in the first place—which events or ideas originally caused us to form that belief? Our theories aren't random. We develop them over time in response to people and events in our life, and they influence how we interpret things. Understanding the specific fear at the bottom of our theories can help us deal not just with the content of our worries, but with the core of anxiety itself.

EXERCISE

THE DOWNWARD ARROW

There's an exercise in cognitive behavioral therapy (CBT) called the *downward arrow technique*. It helps you get to the root of your anxiety-fueled theories about the world. With this exercise, people examine a worry that is causing them problems and ask themselves *why* they're worried about it. What would it mean if a worry came true? How bad would the outcome be? These questions are asked again and again, until the root cause of the worry is exposed.

Let this example guide you. Here, Annaliese is worried about cooking for a party she's hosting.

Surface worry: The meal I'm serving at my dinner party won't turn out right.

Question: If it didn't turn out right, what would it mean to you?

↓

Response: It would mean that I'm a terrible hostess.

↓

Question: And what would that mean to you?

↓

Response: That I can't handle feeding guests and giving them a nice time.

↓

Question: What would that mean?

↓

Response: That I'm a laughingstock! That I can't even do something simple like cook.

↓

(Continued)

Question: And what would that mean?

Response: It's horrible! It means I can't handle anything. Everyone will laugh at me.

Question: So?

Response: They'll leave and won't ever come back. I won't be able to throw any more parties because I won't have any friends.

Notice how Annaliese's worry about ruining the meal is ultimately driven by the fear of being rejected by her friends. Now, rather than just addressing the worry about ruining a meal, Annaliese can confront her larger fear of social rejection.

Now it's your turn. The repeated question "What would it mean?" can be asked as many times as necessary to help you uncover a particular worry's core anxiety. Practice this exercise with different worries.

Question: If it didn't turn out right, what would it mean to you?

↓

Response:

↓

Question: And what would that mean to you?

↓

Response:

↓

Question: What would that mean?

↓

Response:

↓

Question: And what do you think would happen because of this?

↓

Response:

↓

Question: So?

↓

Response:

Homework

Of the exercises you've just completed, which one do you feel helped you the most? Identify ways you can begin to use it in your everyday life as you continue to chip away at anxiety and worry.

Using mindfulness, start bringing mindful attention to your anxiety by simply noticing it. Rather than getting caught in the content of your worries, just note the presence of anxious thoughts in your mind. To do this:

- Pause at various times in your day and take several slow, deep breaths.

- Do you notice any tension or uncomfortable feelings in your body?

- Where are your thoughts? Are they directed at what you're doing, or are you ruminating?

- If you're ruminating, acknowledge that you're caught up in worry and anxiety.

- Don't judge, struggle, or argue with your worries. Just observe your worries without reacting.

- Gently shift your thoughts to something tangible outside of you, like a nearby object or the task you're currently doing.

Anxiety can seem constant and therefore too big to deal with. This self-monitoring process, done throughout each day, will help increase your awareness of when you are worrying. Being mindful of your worries will help you understand their ebbs and flows. From there, you begin strategizing ways to decrease those heightened worrying moments.

Next, in week three, you'll use mindfulness to observe your thoughts and start to loosen their grip on you.

TAKEAWAYS

- We get caught in a cycle of excessive worry known as rumination, which keeps us focused on anxiety.

- Worries are considered irrational when they are about what might possibly happen. Those possibilities, because they're imagined, are endless, intangible, and usually impossible to address.

- Understanding what theories underlie and drive your worries helps reduce anxiety.

- Shifting your thoughts from what is possible (endless and vague) to what is probable (limited and realistic) helps ease worry.

- Use mindfulness to increase your awareness of when you are worrying and when you aren't.

OBSERVING YOUR THOUGHTS

YOUR WEEK

DAY 1

READ:
The Challenge and The Solution

EXERCISE:
Let Your Thoughts Float Away
(12 minutes)

DAY 5

EXERCISE:
Reflection

DAY 2

EXERCISE:
Let Your Thoughts Float Away
(15 Minutes)

EXERCISE:
Observe Your Thoughts Floating
Away During the Day

DAY 6

EXERCISE:
I'm Having the Thought That . . .
(10 minutes)

DAY 3

EXERCISE:
Thinking About vs.
Experiencing: Written Exercise
(20 Minutes)

DAY 7

EXERCISE:
I'm Having the Thought That . . .
(15 minutes)

HOMEWORK

EXERCISE:
Nighttime Reflection

DAY 4

EXERCISE:
Thinking About vs.
Experiencing: Mindfulness
Meditation (12 minutes)

DAY 1

The Challenge

"Never jump into a pile of leaves with a wet sucker."

—LINUS VAN PELT (CHARLES M. SCHULTZ)

Our thoughts can be as sticky as a wet sucker. Wherever we go, there they are, and because they're sticky, we can't pull away. We elaborate on them, taking a single thought and often making it bigger and bigger until it threatens to overwhelm us. Anxious thoughts can distract us from our tasks and interfere with our ability to enjoy the things around us—people, places, and events—that make up our world. We've jumped into the pile of leaves that is our life with our sticky thoughts firmly in hand.

Because our thoughts are sticky, they attract other thoughts and feelings like anxiety and sadness, then those thoughts attract more, until we're positively covered in distracting, sticky thoughts. If they're anxious, unpleasant thoughts, we may try to shake them off but find we can't. They're stuck firm, and the more we struggle with them, the more they cling.

Our thoughts can make us suffer with anxiety, fear, and worry because they seem so *real*. Our thoughts are compelling, often even more compelling than what's going on around us. But as we've seen, our thoughts often aren't as realistic as they appear to us to be. Still, it's hard to remember this in the moment, which is why anxious thoughts can take over so quickly.

We have a thought: *My stomach hurts again today.*

The thought is sticky, so wherever we go, there it is. *Man. It really hurts. It's so bad that I can't stop thinking about it. Something must be really wrong with me.*

Over time, as the thought sticks with us, it begins to attract other thoughts. *This is the third time this week I've had a stomachache—that's not normal. I wonder if I have an ulcer.*

The sticky thought attracts more thoughts, and drives our anxiety ever forward. *Maybe I'm bleeding internally. I should go to the doctor. But I don't want to go through a bunch of expensive tests just to learn that it's nothing.*

Thankfully, there is a powerful solution to this problem of anxious thoughts, a way to reroute your worry car. Let's look at some ways to unstick you from your thoughts.

HOW DO YOU THINK? NEGATIVE THOUGHT PATTERNS

Cognitive behavioral therapy (CBT) is a research-based approach to mental health that focuses on our thoughts and how they impact what we do and how we feel. CBT teaches that we all have a variety of automatic negative thought patterns that affect how we interpret the world. When these negative thought patterns come to dominate how we think, our anxiety can spiral out of control.

There are multiple automatic negative thought patterns at work in anxiety. These three are particularly problematic:

- **Black-and-white thinking.** It's also known as all-or-nothing thinking. When we think in absolutes, there is no room for alternate ideas. You might believe that because you've had anxiety for a long time you'll *never* be able to reduce it.

- **Overgeneralizing.** This involves taking one problem and exaggerating it, inflating it so it applies to everything. One mistake at work means that you're incompetent at everything.

- **Jumping to conclusions.** With this negative belief, you might mind read, "knowing" that someone wouldn't go out on a date with you, or you might fortune tell, "knowing" what negative thing will happen down the road.

When you observe your thoughts, noticing them without judging them, you might begin to notice patterns emerging. Do you tend to be a black-and-white thinker? Do you mind-read, assuming you know what someone is thinking? Pay attention to the content of your thoughts as well as the style, or pattern, that drives them. That will help you catch yourself and shift the nature of what you're thinking.

The Solution:
Seeing Our Thoughts Objectively

Our sticky thoughts collect more thoughts, but why does this happen so quickly? Why is it that we can be noticing a stomachache one minute, and the next be calling our doctor, convinced that we have a bleeding ulcer? In part, it's because we don't typically spend much time examining the qualities of our thoughts or evaluating how realistic they are—we just have them, and then we react.

Learning to look at your thoughts more objectively will allow you to gradually unstick yourself from them, which can be very liberating! Recognizing thoughts for what they are—passing impressions and ideas that will soon be replaced by the next thing that crosses your mind—can help break the habit of mistaking thought for reality. You'll be observing and identifying your anxious thoughts as you do the exercises in this chapter.

To get us started in this process, let's look at some common misconceptions about thoughts.

Unlike emotions, thoughts are factual. FALSE! Thoughts are not facts, though that's easy to forget. Humans have a tendency to blindly believe in all of our thoughts. However, most of the time we can't trust our thoughts to be accurate and unbiased. Take this example of how thoughts can lead you astray: Imagine walking down a hallway at work. You pass your boss and greet her, but she doesn't even glance in your direction. Your anxious thoughts tell you that you've done something wrong and made her angry, that you might even be fired. You spend the day worrying yourself sick. What your thoughts don't know is that your boss had been summoned by her boss, and she was on her way to an important meeting. Preoccupied, she didn't hear you greet her. Your thoughts felt true to you, but in fact they were false.

Our thoughts about events around us accurately reflect the events themselves.
FALSE! Our thoughts about what is happening around us aren't the same as the actual events happening around us. Our thoughts are interpretations of what's happening, not objective recordings of events. But our minds often give thoughts and reality equal weight, which contributes to anxiety. For example, you see your partner embracing someone else. Your thoughts race with worry, telling you that your partner might be having an affair. In truth, this person you love is comforting a coworker whose dog died yesterday. The event and your anxious thoughts about the event are different things.

Our thoughts fill in the gap between what people say and what people mean.

FALSE! Our thoughts try to fill in gaps, but many times there aren't gaps to fill. Or if there are, our thoughts can't know what is supposed to be in the gaps.

Watching Your Thoughts Float Away

All of our attention is given to our anxiety when we battle against our worries. So instead of following your thoughts, arguing with them, or believing them, separate yourself from them. Put a little distance between yourself and your anxious thoughts by watching them float away. Let them come (because no matter how hard you resist, anxious thoughts still pop into our heads) and then let them float right on by. They can't stick to you because you're not engaging with them.

EXERCISE
LET YOUR THOUGHTS FLOAT AWAY (12 MINUTES)

Do this mindfulness meditation and learn how to simply watch your thoughts float away.

1. Get comfortable. Sit or lie in a comfortable position.

2. Set your timer for 12 minutes.

3. Close your eyes and take some slow deep breaths, in and out.

4. Visualize yourself on a bright, sunny day sitting in a meadow, surrounded by dandelions that have gone to seed and become round, white, fuzzy puffs.

5. Visualize yourself picking a dandelion and holding it in front of your face.

6. When a thought comes, picture that thought outside of you on the dandelion.

7. Inhale slowly and deeply, and exhale strongly, blowing the white seeds, your thoughts, into the breeze. (Note: Even though the dandelion is visualized, do breathe deeply in and out as if actually blowing away the seeds.)

8. Observe your thoughts floating away, up into the sky and out of sight. Don't follow them or try to force them out of your head. Just watch them float.

9. "Pick" a new flower and repeat the process until the timer sounds. Continue longer if you wish.

10. Your thoughts might come faster than you are blowing them away, especially at first. That's okay. Keep breathing, blowing, and watching your thoughts float away.

11. Anxiety often prevents us from having fun, so let's add a playful component to this exercise. Instead of visualizing a dandelion puff, physically blow bubbles and watch as your thoughts float and pop away.

DAY 2

LET YOUR THOUGHTS FLOAT AWAY (15 MINUTES)

Let this practice sink in. Today, repeat the exercise, extending your meditation time by a few minutes.

EXERCISE

OBSERVE YOUR THOUGHTS FLOATING AWAY DURING THE DAY

The previous exercise makes a great formal mindfulness meditation. You can also make this mindfulness exercise work even better for you by doing it casually and informally many times throughout each day. Whether you're on the train, in a work meeting, or just getting ready for bed, if you notice your thoughts racing with worry, pause and take slow, deep breaths. Visualize your thoughts floating away on the cottony white dandelion seeds or airy bubbles. You can do it quietly in a matter of minutes, and it will allow you to separate from your thoughts by observing them float away right during an anxious moment.

Where and when can you observe your thoughts floating away? What was the thought you observed passing by? List several examples below.

In my car, stuck in traffic or at a red light.

Had the thought, "I'm going to be late!"

_____

_____

_____

_____

_____

_____

Thinking About vs. Experiencing

Anxiety can trick us into believing our thoughts are reality. When we're feeling anxious, we struggle to distinguish what we're actually experiencing and what our thoughts are projecting. This next mindfulness exercise is designed to help you practice separating your thoughts about your experiences from the lived reality of those experiences.

EXERCISE

THINKING ABOUT VS. EXPERIENCING (10 MINUTES)

1. Sit in a chair with your feet planted flat on the floor. You may wear shoes or socks, or go barefoot. Turn your attention to your feet. You will naturally have thoughts about your feet and the exercise. Turn off all distractions such as your cell phone and music. Set your timer for 10 minutes and let your thoughts about your feet bubble up naturally.

2. Once the timer is up, grab your notebook. What are some of those thoughts? Write down anything that comes to mind.

I left my shoes on. I hope they're clean.

My shoes are red. They make my feet look big. I shouldn't have bought them.

3. Now look back at your thoughts. When you were having those thoughts, you didn't get to fully experience the moment you were in. Next, we'll try a different approach. Set your timer for 20 minutes, and once again, plant your feet on the floor. This time, let your thoughts float away and simply notice the *experience* of your feet while sitting like this.

Where are your feet at the moment?

_____

_____

How do they feel?

_____

_____

What is it like to wiggle your toes? To curl them under?

_____

_____

What is under your feet? How does it feel?

_____

_____

What does it feel like to slide your feet?

_____

_____

Understanding the difference between thinking about something and actually experiencing it can help reduce the power of anxious thoughts. Divert your attention from the thoughts inside your head to what is real around you. Pay attention on purpose. That is, shift your attention away from your worries (*My feet look big in these shoes and I shouldn't have bought them.*) to what you're doing in the moment (*My feet are resting on a hardwood floor, and when I shuffle them, they slide smoothly.*) Doing this repeatedly, whenever you notice anxiety, will train your brain to become more mindful.

EXERCISE

THINKING ABOUT VS. EXPERIENCING: MINDFULNESS MEDITATION (15 MINUTES)

1. Set your timer for 15 minutes.

2. Sit in a chair with your feet flat on the floor. Place a small ball near your toes.

3. Close your eyes and take a slow deep breath, in and out.

4. Notice the floor beneath your feet. Tap your feet several times and notice the feel and the sound.

5. With your eyes closed, find the ball with a foot. Pull it toward you. Feel the muscles of your leg work.

6. Place your left foot on top of the ball. Roll the ball under your foot five times. How does it feel?

7. Place your right foot on top of the ball. Roll the ball under your foot five times. How does it feel? Does it feel different than it did with your left foot, or the same?

8. Pass the ball between your feet. Notice how your muscles move. How are you keeping the ball from rolling away?

9. Reach down and pick up the ball with your hands. Sit up straight.

10. Squeeze the ball in each hand, and toss it back and forth. How does it feel different than it did with your feet? Is anything the same?

11. Continue experiencing the ball and just noticing it until your timer sounds.

DAY 5

REFLECTION

What differences do you notice between thinking about something versus simply experiencing something? How do these differences impact your life?

_____

_____

_____

_____

_____

_____

_____

_____

_____

_____

_____

_____

_____

_____

_____

_____

_____

Separating Thoughts and Feelings

We often confuse thoughts for feelings and get stuck in the messy back and forth between them.

While it can seem as though thoughts and feelings are nearly the same, that's not actually the case. Feelings are emotional states—like fear—that are often closely aligned with physical responses and bodily sensations—like a racing heart or sweaty palms. Thoughts give our feelings life and power by interpreting them, developing them, and ruminating on them. Consider these examples:

Feelings	Thoughts
I *feel* upset because my daughter and I argued this morning.	I *am* so upset because I had a fight with my daughter again this morning. She never respects me. I really messed up as a mother.
I *feel* anxious because the sellers of the house I love might not accept my offer.	I *am* anxious because I might not get the house I want. I don't want any other house. I need this house because of the good schools in the neighborhood. If the sellers don't accept my offer, it will be a disaster for the whole family.

Feelings are the product of a situation, whereas thoughts are stories created by our minds and can run wild and turn into big problems.

I'M HAVING THE THOUGHT THAT . . . (10 MINUTES)

This mindfulness exercise will help you separate your feelings from your thoughts.

1. Sit or lie in a comfortable position.

2. Set your timer for 10 minutes.

3. Close your eyes and take a slow deep breath, in and out.

4. Tune in to your thoughts. Just let them arise and be.

5. When you notice an anxious thought, reframe it. Use the phrase, "I'm having the thought that . . . "

6. So "I screwed up and ruined this relationship," becomes "I'm having the thought that I screwed up and ruined this relationship because . . . "

7. Reframe your thoughts in this way until your alarm sounds.

DAY 7

I'M HAVING THE THOUGHT THAT . . . (15 MINUTES)

Repeat the mindfulness exercise you did yesterday, but extend it just a few more minutes.

Homework

MINDFULNESS ON THE GO

 Every day, use at least one of the previous mindfulness exercises to observe your thoughts. While these can of course be done while seated or lying down as a timed mindfulness meditation, they can also be incorporated into your daily routine as quick ways to shift your thoughts.

As you go about your day, wherever you are and whatever you are doing, become aware of your anxious thoughts and observe them, unsticking yourself in that moment. Catch yourself ruminating then shift your thoughts as you do in the previous mindfulness meditation exercises.

EXERCISE

NIGHTTIME REFLECTION

At the end of the day, grab your notebook, curl up in a blanket, and reflect on your thoughts and mindful observation of them.

- What were some of your ruminations about today?
- Is there a pattern to them?
- What difference did you notice as you did this?
- How will you continue to unstick yourself tomorrow?

TAKEAWAYS

- Our anxious thoughts are sticky, and the more we struggle against them, the more they hold on to us.

- Being stuck to our thoughts is one of the things that drives anxiety.

- Thoughts aren't always true or accurate.

- Our thoughts about events aren't the same as the actual events.

- In truth, our thoughts aren't who we are and instead are just mental events.

- We don't always choose our thoughts, but we can choose how we respond to them.

- Recognizing and simply observing our thoughts is the key to unsticking ourselves from anxious worries and ruminations.

WEEK FOUR

SOCIAL ANXIETY

WEEK 4

YOUR WEEK

DAY 1

READ:
The Challenge

EXERCISE:
Reflection

READ:
The Solution

EXERCISE:
Self-Assessment

EXERCISE:
Reflection

DAY 2

EXERCISE:
Working with Uncertainties

EXERCISE:
Where Did This All Start?

DAY 3

EXERCISE:
Intolerance of Uncertainty in
Unfamiliar Situations

EXERCISE:
Reflection

DAY 4

EXERCISE:
Intolerance of Uncertainty in
Familiar Situations

EXERCISE:
Reflection

DAY 5

EXERCISE:
Practice Tolerance of
Uncertainty (Part One)

DAY 6

EXERCISE:
Practice Uncertainty Acceptance
(Part Two)

EXERCISE:
Move Toward a Goal with Action

DAY 7

EXERCISE:
Acting Despite Uncertainty

HOMEWORK

The Challenge

Do you ever feel uncomfortable or nervous about meeting new people? Have you ever worried that your friends are watching you and passing judgment? Do you fear that people won't think you're smart or competent, or that they just plain won't like you? Have you ever been afraid of being embarrassed or even humiliated around other people? Maybe sometimes you've been scared that people will see your discomfort and anxiety, and judge you negatively for that, too.

This particular kind of anxiety, relating to other people and their perceptions of you, is called social anxiety, and it can really limit people's lives. If you have ever experienced social anxiety, you're not alone. Social anxiety, which exists on a wide spectrum from uncomfortable shyness to something called avoidant personality disorder, is extremely common. It's one of the most common forms of anxiety, and many people who don't have problems with anxiety generally still experience social anxiety and discomfort from time to time.

Social anxiety can show up in lots of different situations. This partial list indicates where you might feel anxious about being judged negatively:

- Places where there are a lot of people
- Parties
- At school (cafeteria, classrooms, bathrooms, hallways)
- Meeting someone for the first time
- Going on a date
- Being assertive/standing up for yourself
- Eating or drinking around others
- Any place where you feel like you're on display or the center of attention

REFLECTION

There is no one way to experience social anxiety. My own social anxiety always used to strike in situations related to my performance. For me, social anxiety was tied to a strong sense of perfectionism and what's known as the imposter syndrome: believing that others "knew" that I was actually incompetent and were judging me for it. There is no one way to have social anxiety. What is social anxiety like for you? Is it limited to one or two situations, or is it wide ranging? Pause here to reflect on social situations that are anxiety provoking in any way. On the lines below, list circumstances that lead to social anxiety, and describe how this anxiety is getting in the way of your lifestyle or happiness.

Most people do experience a degree of social anxiety now and then, such as when they feel nervous upon entering a room full of people, for example. How much would you say that social anxiety is blocking you from living fully and creating the quality of life you want to live? On a scale from 1 to 10, with 1 being not at all and 10 being so severe that you have extreme difficulty leaving your house, where would you rate your social anxiety? Limited instances that have a low rating, likely a two or three on the scale, aren't much of a problem. Social anxiety becomes a problem when it causes you to change your behavior in a way that prevents you from moving forward in your life, because you are engaging in counterproductive strategies, such as:

- **Avoidance.** Going to great lengths to skip an event or social situation that will cause you anxiety.

- **Escape.** Attending the social situation but leaving early.

- **Safety-seeking.** Using self-protective behaviors to get through an anxiety-provoking situation.

The Solution: Managing Your Intolerance of Uncertainty

There are basic ways to examine social anxiety to understand its impact on our lives, so we can then determine solutions for breaking free from its influence. One solution to the problems presented by social anxiety lies in a concept known as *intolerance of uncertainty*. Intolerance of uncertainty simply means that we humans don't like the unknown—whether that's new people, or events with unpredictable outcomes. We hate feeling uncertain of what might happen to us; we equate it with danger. Research has shown that intolerance of uncertainty contributes greatly to worry and generalized anxiety (Berenbaum et al. 2008; Leahy 2017). It follows that the less tolerant you are of uncertainty, the more anxious you'll feel—because life is full of unpredictable circumstances and unforeseen outcomes.

If you are a person with high levels of anxiety, it's likely that you also have a low tolerance for uncertainty. Intolerance of uncertainty plays a clear role in social anxiety, too, because people can be pretty unpredictable. When you meet a new person, or walk into a new social environment, you really can't predict with very much certainty how people will react to you or how things will go. For many of us, intolerance of uncertainty can become socially limiting, because we will just choose to avoid new people and activities rather than experience that painful anxiety spike.

When we live with social anxiety, we avoid, escape, and engage in safety-seeking behaviors as a way to handle our intolerance of uncertainty. While we're very certain that we will be judged, we're uncertain about the degree to which we'll be judged, by whom, and just how negative the consequences will be.

The following examples illustrate how social anxiety and its difficulties relate to intolerance of uncertainty.

The Uncertainty	How It's Limiting Your Life (Avoidance, Escape, and/or Safety-Seeking)	How Much of a Problem Is This Causing? (1 to 10 Scale)
I don't know how that stranger at the party is going to react to me.	Escape (I left early so I didn't have to talk to him.)	6 (I'm not much of a party person, but I would like to enjoy and stay at the ones I go to.)
I have a date, but I don't know how it will go or what she'll think of me.	Avoidance (I made up an excuse and canceled.)	10 (I keep canceling dates or avoiding asking people, but I'd really like to date and meet someone special.)
How much of a fool did I make of myself in that meeting? I don't know if I said the right things or said too much or too little.	Safety-seeking (I shut down when I started to feel judged and started to take notes. I didn't talk again or even look up.)	8 (I'm going to work, but I feel anxious and sick. I don't know how much longer I can do it. I'm losing sleep over it.)

Now that you know a bit more about the intolerance of uncertainty and social anxiety, and have begun to reflect on how it impacts you, you're ready to go deeper. The following exercises are designed to help you address the avoidance, escape, and safety behaviors you use to avoid or minimize social anxiety. Eliminating uncertainty in life is impossible, but you can improve your ability to tolerate life's uncertainties. Taking charge of your life, decisions, and emotions is definitely possible—even with the unpredictable nature of people and daily events. With the strategies and exercises in this chapter, you can learn how to reduce social anxiety and increase your willingness to move forward despite uncertainty.

How Well Do You Tolerate Uncertainty?

EXERCISE

SELF-ASSESSMENT

This questionnaire is designed to help you assess your own intolerance of uncertainty and see how much it's interfering in your social interactions. Read each statement and consider how much you agree with it (how much it affects your life). Check the appropriate box. Using the descriptions below to guide you, check the box that best describes your response to each example of social uncertainty.

- ✓ Doesn't Bother Me
- ✓ Somewhat Bothers Me (I feel anxious and uncomfortable, but I can do it)
- ✓ Bothers Me Quite a Bit (I feel really anxious, but I can do it with some avoidance, escape, or safety behaviors)
- ✓ Severely Restricts Me (My anxiety is so extreme that I completely avoid the situation or escape in near panic)

Examples of Social Uncertainty	DOESN'T BOTHER ME	SOMEWHAT BOTHERS ME	BOTHERS ME QUITE A BIT	SEVERELY RESTRICTS ME
Feeling like you can't read someone's body language.				
You were invited to a party, but you don't know who is going to be there.				
You're in the middle of a group conversation.				
Arriving to a class and all of the back row seats are taken, so you have to sit in one of the front rows.				
You're invited to a potluck where you don't know anyone, and the host is requesting everyone bring a dish.				
You're at an event where people are playing games or dancing.				
At work, you have an idea or suggestion for a coworker.				
At school, sitting and talking with classmates.				
An acquaintance or friend gives you a strange look.				
Shopping for groceries and heading to checkout.				

(Continued)

Examples of Social Uncertainty	DOESN'T BOTHER ME	SOMEWHAT BOTHERS ME	BOTHERS ME QUITE A BIT	SEVERELY RESTRICTS ME
Grocery shopping and using the automated self-checkout feature.				
Someone asks for your input on a topic or concern.				
Having goals or aspirations, socially or career-wise.				
You get flushed cheeks when you get embarrassed.				
You need to continuously ask people if they're mad at you.				
Someone gives you a compliment or praise, but you don't know if they're sincere.				
Overthinking and wondering if others are judging you.				
Sitting or standing with other parents at your child's school function.				
Meeting new people.				
The gifts you give friends, family, and colleagues.				

To score your assessment, assign numbers to your answers according to their category:

- Doesn't Bother Me = 0
- Somewhat Bothers Me = 1
- Bothers Me Quite a Bit = 2
- Severely Restricts Me = 3

Now, add up your numbers. Here's how to interpret them:

If Your Score Is...	...Your Intolerance of Uncertainty Likely Means
0–15	You're not very concerned about what people might be thinking of you. Your actions aren't affected by the possibility of being judged. Social anxiety isn't much of a problem for you.
16–30	You likely feel uncomfortable in many social settings because you're not sure if people are judging you or not.
31–45	Your anxiety flares up in social settings because you don't know what people are thinking about you, but you assume it's negative.
46–60	Your severe anxiety is getting in the way of your ability to actually enjoy life. You don't know exactly how people are judging you, but you "know" they're doing it, and you "know" it's terrible. You avoid others and their judgments so much that you're practically trapped in your home.

EXERCISE

WHERE DID THIS ALL START?

In your journal, reflect on your score. Does it seem accurate? Return to the chart and put a check ✓ in the left-hand column beside those situations that are the most bothersome for you. Write some specific examples of how your intolerance of uncertainty in social situations is negatively affecting your life. How would you like things to be different?

EXERCISE

WORKING WITH UNCERTAINTIES

Next, let's look at how you can begin to better tolerate uncertainty to reduce social anxiety. The column on the left lists some social settings where you could experience intolerance of uncertainty. The right columns are blank for you to reflect on the particular situations that are challenging to you. Concentrate on those situations that cause you anxiety—it's okay if you don't fill in every social situation, as they may not all apply to you. The example shows you how to get started.

Anxiety-Provoking Situation	WHAT'S MY UNCERTAINTY?	WHAT'S THE WORST THAT WOULD HAPPEN IF I'M RIGHT?	WHY DO I WANT TO PUT MYSELF IN THIS SITUATION ANYWAY?	WHAT IS ONE THING I CAN DO TO STAY IN THE SOCIAL SITUATION?
My daughter's back-to-school night.	Other parents will think I'm annoying if I ask questions or too quiet and weird if I don't.	The other parents will tell their kids that we're a strange family and that they can't hang out with my daughter. She'll be ostracized because of me.	It's important to me that I be involved in my daughter's education, and I want her to know that I'm here to support her.	I'll go to the open house. I'll focus on why I'm there: to meet her teachers and see her rooms. I'll do that. I'll think about what the teachers say instead of what I think the other parents are saying.

Anxiety-Provoking Situation	WHAT'S MY UNCERTAINTY?	WHAT'S THE WORST THAT WOULD HAPPEN IF I'M RIGHT?	WHY DO I WANT TO PUT MYSELF IN THIS SITUATION ANYWAY?	WHAT IS ONE THING I CAN DO TO STAY IN THE SOCIAL SITUATION?
Family				
Friends				
School				
Work				
Crowded places, such as long lines at stores				
Parties/ gatherings				
Talking on the phone				

(Continued)

Anxiety-Provoking Situation	WHAT'S MY UNCERTAINTY?	WHAT'S THE WORST THAT WOULD HAPPEN IF I'M RIGHT?	WHY DO I WANT TO PUT MYSELF IN THIS SITUATION ANYWAY?	WHAT IS ONE THING I CAN DO TO STAY IN THE SOCIAL SITUATION?
Giving a presentation				
Chatting with acquaintances				
Small talk with strangers				
Events for your children or grandchildren				

EXERCISE

REFLECTION

Take one of the anxiety-provoking situations you just assessed and write about how the seed for this anxious thought was first planted. What was the incident and when did it happen? How did you react to that moment? How might you approach it differently now?

How Does Intolerance of Uncertainty Show Up?

EXERCISE

INTOLERANCE OF UNCERTAINTY IN UNFAMILIAR SITUATIONS

When it comes to social anxiety, intolerance of uncertainty takes the form of thoughts (*I know everyone here thinks I'm a complete idiot.*) and feelings (*I feel embarrassed. I feel sad.*). As we've seen with avoidance, escape, and safety behaviors, intolerance of uncertainty also very much affects our actions, decisions, and behaviors.

Once we recognize what we are (or aren't) doing to manage our intolerance of uncertainty, we can stop practicing anxious avoidance and start living more positively. This exercise is designed to help you do that.

Today, focus on social anxiety and intolerance of uncertainty that you experience when you're around people you don't know, or when you're in unfamiliar situations. On the left side of the table on page 76, list things you do to avoid or escape situations that cause uncertainty and/or things you do to prevent uncertainty in social situations (safety behaviors). On the right side, rate the level of your social anxiety in each behavior listed. Use a scale from 1 to 10, with 1 representing no anxiety at all and 10 representing severe anxiety. Use the example to get started.

Behaviors I Do to Avoid or Reduce Social Anxiety Due to Intolerance of Uncertainty in Unfamiliar Situations	My Anxiety Level When I'm Doing These Things
In areas with lots of people, I stand as far away from others as I can, and I pretend to use my phone so I don't have to look at anyone.	8

EXERCISE
REFLECTION

Take a look at the anxiety levels you indicated for each behavior. Is your anxiety higher than you want it to be despite avoiding or engaging in safety behavior? In your journal, list several reasons why avoidance, escape, and safety behaviors are not effective solutions in managing intolerance of uncertainty and social anxiety in unfamiliar situations.

EXERCISE

INTOLERANCE OF UNCERTAINTY IN FAMILIAR SITUATIONS

Today's exercise is a continuation of yesterday's. This time, though, you'll focus on the social anxiety you may experience around friends, family, and colleagues, and in familiar situations.

As before, on the left side of the table below, list things you do to reduce your uncertainty in a social situation (safety behaviors). On the right side, rate the level of your social anxiety when engaging in the behavior you listed. Use a scale from 1 to 10, with 1 representing no anxiety at all and 10 representing severe anxiety.

Behaviors I Do to Avoid or Reduce Social Anxiety Due to Intolerance of Uncertainty in Familiar Situations	My Anxiety Level When I'm Doing These Things
I don't know what the people in my book club will think about my comments in our discussions. They might think I'm stupid. So, I just sit there, drink the wine, and be quiet.	9

REFLECTION

This journal reflection is similar to yesterday's, but your focus now is on familiar situations. When you look at the anxiety levels you indicated for each behavior, what do you notice? Is your anxiety higher than you want it to be despite avoiding or engaging in safety behaviors? List several reasons why avoidance, escape, and safety behaviors aren't very effective in helping you successfully manage intolerance of uncertainty and social anxiety in familiar situations.

Practice Tolerance of Uncertainty

The first step to decreasing your anxiety is observing your behavior when you feel worried or anxious. With self-awareness, you give yourself the option of responding differently to anxiety, instead of immediately reacting in your usual way. These new responses, practiced over time, will eventually increase your tolerance of uncertainty, and decrease the anxiety you feel when dealing with life's unpredictability. New behaviors are the foundation of your plan for positive change.

EXERCISE

PRACTICE UNCERTAINTY ACCEPTANCE (PART ONE)

In the left column of the chart on page 80, copy three or four of the behaviors you listed on page 76. In the middle column, write something you could do differently. How can you interact with the people you want or need to without intolerance of uncertainty getting in your way? In the right column, rate your potential anxiety level the way you did in the exercise on page 76.

The anxiety rating is here for a reason. It's to let you know that changing your behavior won't magically eliminate social anxiety, and your anxiety might actually *increase* when you first try a new behavior. This is completely normal and to be expected. Don't think that there's something wrong with you if you feel anxious as you try out new behaviors, and don't give up! If you stick with it, you'll start to experience the benefits of taking positive action.

Behaviors I Do to Avoid or Reduce Social Anxiety Due to Intolerance of Uncertainty	Something Different I Could Do to Be in That Situation Even Though I Don't Know if Others Are Judging Me	My Anxiety Level When I'm Doing These New Things
In places with lots of people, I stand as far away from others as I can, and I pretend to use my phone so I don't have to look at anyone.	I'll put my phone away and look around, practicing open awareness. Each time I'm in a situation with lots of people, I'll stand a little closer to the main area.	7 (or maybe higher because just this idea is making me anxious!)

PRACTICE UNCERTAINTY ACCEPTANCE (PART TWO)

Continue to add to the chart you began yesterday. List things you avoid, escape, or respond to with safety behaviors, and write down the things you could do differently.

EXERCISE

MOVE TOWARD A GOAL WITH ACTION

1. Choose one of your suggestions for something you could do differently, and do it now (in a situation that fits right now). This is the first step for moving past your uncertainty and anxiety by moving toward a goal despite experiencing those emotions.

2. Now, reflect on the experience.

What did you do differently?

_____

_____

_____

How do you think your life will change as you continue to take this action?

_____

_____

_____

What is the difference between getting answers to your uncertainties (e.g., "My boss told me my presentation was great") and changing your actions to tolerate them better?

_____

_____

_____

ACTING DESPITE UNCERTAINTY

 Go more deeply in your journal. *How* can you continue to face uncertainty in social situations and take positive action *anyway*?

Homework

 During weeks one and three, you learned these mindfulness techniques:

- Breath Awareness
- Mindful Eating
- Open Awareness
- Watching Your Thoughts Float Away
- "Thinking About" vs. "Experiencing"
- Separating Thoughts and Feelings

For this week's homework, first consider two situations where intolerance of uncertainty stirs up social anxiety. Next, pick one or two mindfulness exercises to do when you are in those situations. Be intentional about practicing mindfulness when your intolerance of uncertainty and anxiety are high.

Later, reflect in your journal. How difficult was it to engage in mindfulness when you felt anxious? How did it change your thoughts and feelings during the experiences? In what ways was your anxiety better as you practiced mindfulness?

TAKEAWAYS

- Social anxiety involves the fear of being judged, embarrassed, or humiliated.

- Intolerance of uncertainty fuels social anxiety.

- Intolerance of uncertainty involves discomfort with not knowing what people are thinking about us and assuming the worst.

- Intolerance of uncertainty and social anxiety limit our lives when we engage in avoidance, escape, or self-protective behaviors.

- Knowing yourself and the source of your intolerance of uncertainty and social anxiety helps you make positive behavior changes.

- Mindfulness helps us deal with intolerance of uncertainty and social anxiety without needing to avoid, escape, or constantly self-protect in social situations.

WORKING WITH DIFFICULT EMOTIONS

WEEK 5

YOUR WEEK

DAY 1

READ:
The Challenge

EXERCISE:
How Is Avoidance Working in Your Life?

READ:
The Solution

DAY 2

EXERCISE:
Explore and Observe Your Emotions (15 minutes)

EXERCISE:
Reflection on Exploring Difficult Emotions (Part One)

DAY 3

EXERCISE:
Explore and Observe Your Emotions (20 Minutes)

EXERCISE:
Reflection on Exploring Difficult Emotions (Part Two)

DAY 4

EXERCISE:
Inviting Difficult Emotions (15 Minutes)

EXERCISE:
Inviting Your Difficult Emotions

DAY 5

EXERCISE:
Inviting Difficult Emotions (20 Minutes)

EXERCISE:
Reflection on Inviting Your Difficult Emotions

EXERCISE:
Lovingkindness Meditation (5 minutes)

EXERCISE:
Write Your Own Lovingkindness Meditation

DAY 6

EXERCISE:
Lovingkindness Affirmations

DAY 7

HOMEWORK

The Challenge

Unpleasant emotions are a part of the human experience. Sadness, fear, self-doubt, anger, and anxiety are emotions we all experience, sometimes so strongly that they seem to dominate our lives. As we learned at the beginning of this book (Why We Struggle with Anxiety, page 1), we all have a built-in tendency toward avoidance, because the brain is hardwired to avoid painful and unpleasant experiences.

When we encounter something that causes our anxiety to spike, the brain's fight-or-fight response kicks into high gear. The brain does this even when it doesn't perceive a threat. Once the fear response is activated, we will often either fight or flee. Fighting isn't really practical in our society, so we mostly flee.

While the impulse to avoid unpleasant experiences is wired into our brains, avoidance is also a *learned* behavior. We develop troublesome avoidance patterns because when we avoid something that stresses us out, we experience a short burst of relief—which convinces us, at least for a while, that avoidance *works*. Of course, it doesn't really work. Avoidance actually increases anxiety over time, because it reinforces and strengthens our anxious behaviors and thoughts.

Let's consider some examples. Do you recognize any of these avoidant behaviors?

- Calling in sick to work because you are full of self-doubt and afraid that your presentation will go poorly.

- You tell the parents organizing your son's school band fundraiser that you can't make it to the event, because you've argued with one of the parents and are afraid of her confronting you again. You're sad and your son is disappointed, but you feel you just can't go.

- You worry that a work project won't be good enough, so you avoid doing it.

- Because of your anxiety about eating in front of others, you don't go to the Christmas party your friend invited you to. Now you're afraid that you've damaged your friendship.

- You worry that your daughter will be hurt or killed in a car accident someday, so you refuse to teach her to drive.

ANXIETY AND THE BRAIN

Our anxiety and natural desire to avoid unpleasant sensations are hardwired into our entire brain—not just the amygdala, which people commonly associate with the fight-or-flight response. This fear response also involves the hypothalamus, the sympathetic nervous system, and the adrenal-cortical system. But that's not all that's implicated in our anxiety and drive for avoidance.

All of these areas and systems of the brain are involved in our anxiety:

- Neocortex (higher thinking and processing—our anxious thoughts, including our plans and schemes to avoid)

- Limbic system (the emotion center—our anxious feelings, including the desire to avoid)

- Reptilian brain

- Amygdala

- Hypothalamic-pituitary-adrenal axis

- Hippocampus

- Lateral septum

- Hormones and neurotransmitters (such as adrenaline and cortisol—stress and fight/flight)

Anxiety is something we all naturally experience. But we don't have to be controlled by our anxiety—which is what this book is all about! You can learn to manage your brain's natural anxiety responses and take charge of your life again.

HOW IS AVOIDANCE WORKING IN YOUR LIFE?

Now, it's time for you to make it personal. What are some of *your* unique worries, fears, and anxieties? What strategies do you tend to use to avoid the discomfort that comes from these unpleasant thoughts and feelings? Complete this table to develop a deeper understanding of how your avoidance of unpleasant emotions is affecting you. Use the example as a guide.

Unpleasant Emotion or Thought	Avoidance Strategy	Why it Made My Unpleasant Emotions, Thoughts, and Anxieties Worse
Anger at another band parent, anxiety about her confronting me.	Send my cake and extra cookies with my son instead of going to the event.	I am sad that I disappointed my son and missed out on the event. I'm worried that I upset everyone. It will be harder to face them next time.

When you focus on wanting to avoid negative emotions, your attention is on two things: the problem, and what you can do to avoid it. Notice that your focus and attention are *not* on how you can break through the limits and traps, get out of the cycle, and live fully anyway, despite problems.

The Solution: Accepting Our Anxiety

Acceptance of your anxiety is your key to living well. Your anxiety is a part of your life experience, and all the workbooks in the world won't make it disappear entirely. The secret is, you can live a full and satisfying life, even with anxiety present—if you're willing to accept that anxiety is simply going to be present at times.

The idea of happily going about your business, even as your anxiety spikes or causes you discomfort, can seem strange at first. Shouldn't we wait to feel better, *then* start living the life we want? That's a common idea, but it's also an avoidance strategy I call *waiting for someday*. It never works. Problems exist. We feel unpleasant emotions. We have anxieties. But we also have choices. We can choose to continue to avoid our problems and remain stuck, or we can choose to accept them and *move forward anyway*.

Acceptance doesn't mean resignation. It doesn't mean giving up or throwing in the towel. Acceptance is acknowledging that pain and difficulty are there with us, and choosing to bring them along for the ride as we fully inhabit our daily lives.

With acceptance, we are better equipped to ride out life's challenging moments. That's because when we choose to adopt the attitude of acceptance, instead of constantly fighting circumstances or our own emotional state, we can broaden our focus and make room for new thoughts and emotions, like contentment or joy. Struggling and avoiding keep our attention focused on anxiety and problems.

Acceptance is both an attitude *and* a behavior, and it doesn't always come easy. The good news is that in learning to focus our attention mindfully on different aspects of our experience, we increase our ability to be present with things other than anxiety—like our kids or a fun party—even when anxiety is there, too.

Exploring Difficult Emotions

The purpose of this exercise is to help you become more deeply aware of your difficult emotions so you can start to learn to accept them. In this meditation, you will simply notice these emotions, rather than engage, argue with, or try to "solve" them (emotions aren't something that have a solution). As you do this, just observe what emotions arise, rather than judging them, or yourself.

EXERCISE

EXPLORE AND OBSERVE YOUR EMOTIONS (15 MINUTES)

1. Get comfortable by sitting or lying down.

2. Set your timer for 15 minutes.

3. Breathe in slowly, through your nose. Hear the air moving into your body.

4. Pause briefly and feel your body hold the air.

5. Exhale slowly through your mouth, feeling the air pass across your lips as your belly relaxes.

6. Continue breathing deeply for several breaths, feeling your body react to the air coming in and going out.

7. Still breathing slowly and deeply, now visualize a gently flowing stream. You notice big leaves floating on the current, and you simply observe them passing.

8. A few of the leaves carry orbs, softly glowing, translucent, and pulsing with vibrant golds, blues, greens, and purples. Curious, you reach over and pluck one out. It's pleasantly warm. Leaves continue to float gently by, but now your attention is on the glowing orb in your palms.

9. As you study the orb, you notice something shimmering inside it. Looking closer, you see that there is a word floating inside the orb. You read it. The word is an emotion, and it's one of your most problematic feelings. What is it? Fear? Jealousy? Just notice, don't react.

10. Notice how the orb now feels in your hand. What is its temperature? Texture? Is it light, or is it heavy? Again, just observe. Don't try to force a description or change how it feels.

11. Starting at your feet, scan your body very slowly. Notice any sensations that arise from holding the orb of emotion in your hand. Where do you notice the feeling of this emotion? Your abdomen? Your chest? Your jaw? Your head? Elsewhere? Stay with the feeling and let it be. Just accept its presence.

12. How is your mind reacting to this emotion? Again, don't try to change anything. Accept any thoughts or feelings by allowing them to arise, then float away down the river.

13. Remain in your position, breathing deeply, noticing your physical body and mind, and accept the presence of your emotion.

14. When your timer dings, take several slow, deep, breaths, and gently open your eyes. Notice how you feel, and thank yourself for the experience of acceptance of your emotion and mindfulness of the moment.

EXERCISE

REFLECTION ON EXPLORING DIFFICULT EMOTIONS (PART ONE)

What was this experience like for you? Write down the name of the emotion, and describe where you felt it in your body as well as what it felt like. What was it like to allow yourself to have thoughts and then just let them float away?

_____

_____

_____

_____

_____

_____

_____

DAY 3

EXERCISE

EXPLORE AND OBSERVE YOUR EMOTIONS (20 MINUTES)

Return to the meditation exercise you did yesterday. Repeat the exercise, this time exploring a different unpleasant emotion and staying with the meditation just a few minutes longer.

EXERCISE

REFLECTION ON EXPLORING DIFFICULT EMOTIONS (PART TWO)

What was this experience like for you today? Was it different than yesterday? If so, how? Write down the name of the emotion you chose today, and describe where you felt it in your body as well as what it felt like. What was it like to allow yourself to have thoughts and then just let them float away? How was this experience of observation, acceptance, and being in the present moment with the unpleasant emotion?

_____

_____

_____

_____

_____

_____

_____

_____

_____

_____

IF YOU START TO FEEL OVERWHELMED

When you first do this mindfulness exercise, you might feel your emotions pretty strongly. That's okay. Sticking with them, rather than looking for an escape, is an important part of the exercise. However, painful emotions can sometimes feel overwhelming. If you start to feel like your emotions are more than you can manage, you may gently open your eyes and turn your attention to what you see around you. Observe the objects in the room while you continue to breathe deeply. Once you feel calmer, you can end your session and plan to revisit the exercise later.

Sometimes facing unpleasant emotions temporarily increases anxiety and might even trigger a panic attack. If you find yourself overwhelmed by anxiety even after you stop the exercise, do one or more of these things to take care of yourself in the moment:

- Take slow, deep breaths, as many as you need to in order to feel calm.

- While breathing slowly and deeply, visualize a peaceful, soothing place. Maybe you feel calm while hiking in the woods. Or perhaps you enjoy a quiet walk on a lake shore or even the ocean. Maybe the most peaceful place you know is in your home.

- You can pair deep breathing with aromatherapy, using a candle or essential oil diffuser to infuse the air with a calming, relaxing scent such as lavender, rose, bergamot, or chamomile.

- Drink a soothing, noncaffeinated tea. As with the aromas, lavender and chamomile are great herbs for reducing anxiety, along with passionflower, hawthorn, kava, ginseng, and lemon balm.

- Ground yourself. This means centering your body by connecting to something solid. Sit in a chair and plant your feet firmly on the floor while placing your hands on the armrests or seat of the chair. You can also stand with your feet planted on the ground and your back pressed against a wall. Ground yourself physically in a way that feels comfortable.

- Notice negative thoughts and replace them with simple positive ones. *I can't handle this* becomes *I am handling this right now, I am doing things in this moment to get through it, and I know this panic will pass.*

Letting yourself experience and accept strong emotions helps you deescalate strong feelings.

Inviting Difficult Emotions

This mindfulness meditation is another exercise designed to help you practice accepting difficult emotions rather than avoiding them. By acknowledging a difficult emotion and viewing it more objectively, you're opening up some breathing space between it and you. Eventually, a hard situation or feeling can become just another transient event in your life, like a headache, rather than a scary beast that threatens to take over. This transformation of perspective allows you to let in more positive things and live more fully.

EXERCISE

INVITING DIFFICULT EMOTIONS (15 MINUTES)

In this mindfulness exercise, choose an uncomfortable emotion that is relatively mild. Please don't try to confront a trauma or other deep-seated pain.

1. Get comfortable by sitting or lying down.

2. Set your timer for 15 minutes.

3. Breathe in slowly, through your nose. Hear the air moving into your body.

4. Pause briefly and feel your body hold the air.

5. Exhale slowly through your mouth, feeling the air pass across your lips as your belly relaxes.

6. Continue to breathe deeply for several breaths, feeling your body react to the air coming in and going out.

7. Still breathing slowly and deeply, call to mind a situation or person that's bothering you. What emotion arises? If more than one emotion surfaces, choose the strongest one right now.

8. Notice how you react. Scan your body for tension, and breathe into the tense areas.

9. Invite your unpleasant emotion to sit beside you or across from you. Ask it to breathe with you.

10. Visualize having tea with it. Hear the sound the tea makes as you pour it into beautiful cups. Watch the steam rise and curl. Hand a cup to your emotion, and take a sip of your own.

11. Simply sit and sip tea with the emotion. Don't struggle, argue, or fight with it.

12. Scan your body. Beginning with your feet and moving up bit by bit, notice how you feel. Breathe into any areas that feel tense, cramped, or otherwise uncomfortable.

13. Remain in your position, breathing deeply and noticing your whole self sitting with your unpleasant emotion. You're letting it be and sipping tea with it.

14. When your timer dings, take several slow deep breaths, and gently open your eyes. Notice how you feel, and thank yourself for the experience of acceptance of your emotion and mindfulness of the moment.

EXERCISE
INVITING YOUR DIFFICULT EMOTIONS

Let's take another look at inviting in difficult emotions and staying with them in the moment.

Choose a different problematic situation or uncomfortable emotion, one that is more complex than the emotion you chose for the meditation.

Describe this situation or emotion:

_____

_____

_____

_____

How have you been avoiding it?

_____

_____

_____

_____

How has this avoidance gotten in the way of your lifestyle and happiness?

_____

_____

_____

_____

_____

_____

_____

_____

_____

Now, set this book aside and close your eyes. Breathe deeply. Let this emotion come into your full awareness. Simply sit with it for several minutes, feeling it in your body and mind. How did doing this affect you?

As you work through these exercises, what difficulties do you imagine might arise? How will you move through those difficulties?

DAY 5

INVITING DIFFICULT EMOTIONS (20 MINUTES)

Return to yesterday's meditation. Repeat the exercise and invite in a different uncomfortable emotion, this time meditating with it for just a few minutes more.

EXERCISE

REFLECTION ON INVITING YOUR DIFFICULT EMOTIONS

On a scale from 1 to 10, with 1 being not at all and 10 being completely, to what degree do you feel that you can continue to invite your difficult emotions into your life, in these meditation exercises, and as you go about each day? _____

Why did you choose the number you did?

_____

_____

_____

_____

_____

_____

What would it take for you to move up the scale to the next number?

_____

_____

_____

_____

_____

_____

_____

What would the advantages be for you if you revoked your invitation and continued to avoid?

_____

_____

_____

_____

What are the advantages of inviting and accepting your difficult emotions and being fully present in your moments despite these negative feelings?

_____

_____

_____

_____

Bringing Compassion to Difficult Emotions

So often, our uncomfortable emotions and negative thoughts are directed at ourselves. This is true for everyone, and it's especially true for people living with anxiety. Anxiety and self-criticism are partners in crime. And self-criticism can be dangerously toxic.

Breaking the habit of harmful self-criticism requires changing the way we perceive ourselves. Lovingkindness is a progressive approach to managing our difficult emotions, anxieties, and worries. Lovingkindness isn't just a personal practice; it extends to others in our lives and our larger communities—a full lovingkindness practice encompasses the whole world. Cultivating compassion teaches us to accept our anxiety, our difficult emotions, and anything else that's standing in the way of our ability to live the quality life we desire.

LOVINGKINDNESS MEDITATION (5 MINUTES)

Try this lovingkindness meditation as a way to practice accepting yourself and your challenges. If you can't remember all the phrases I've provided here, that's okay. The essence of this kind of meditation is the benevolent wish for health and well-being, for yourself and all life on earth.

1. Get comfortable by sitting or lying down.

2. Set your timer for 5 minutes.

3. Breathe in slowly through your nose. Hear the air moving into your body.

4. Pause briefly and feel your body hold the air.

5. Exhale slowly through your mouth, feeling the air pass across your lips as your belly relaxes.

6. Continue to breathe deeply for several breaths, feeling your body react to the air coming in and going out.

7. Say the following statements aloud as you contemplate the words:

- May I live peacefully alongside all of my emotions and anxiety.
- May I accept what is happening in my life, moment by moment.
- May my acceptance give me courage to face, not avoid, situations and people.
- May I live my life fully and freely, enjoying my life even when I feel anxious.
- May my loved ones enjoy this acceptance and freedom, too.
- May all of the world's people accept their anxieties and emotions, living fully.

WRITE YOUR OWN LOVINGKINDNESS MEDITATION

This type of meditation involves a series of simple sentences (any number) beginning with "May . . . " What would you like to see improve regarding your anxiety? What would the best version of life look like without anxiety? Write your intentions in the form of a lovingkindness meditation.

DAY 6

Do at least two lovingkindness meditations today, using either the scripted one from yesterday, or the one that you wrote in the workbook exercise, for five minutes.

LOVINGKINDNESS AFFIRMATIONS

Lovingkindness statements can be done in meditation, as you've been doing in the lovingkindess meditations. They can also be used as a form of affirmation. Affirmations are short statements said throughout the day that change our thoughts. They can be said quietly in your head or out loud. You can memorize them or write them down, placing them in prominent places—on your desk at work, on the refrigerator at home, or on your car's dashboard. Here, lovingkindness statements used as affirmations will reinforce our acceptance of anxiety and unpleasant emotions.

In your notebook, start and maintain a running list of lovingkindness statements, your goals and desires for your life. You can start off the list by including the statements you already wrote for your meditation exercise. Keep going! You should aim to accumulate a long list of statements of lovingkindness.

DAY 7

Homework

Acceptance can seem difficult at first, but it is one of the most powerful tools to help you manage your anxiety and avoidance. With practice, you'll eventually learn how powerful acceptance can be for your personal growth. In my own progression, acceptance is one of my core mind-sets to this day. This attitude and way of life has reduced my anxiety and improved my ability to live well, even when tense moments flare up. These reflective questions will help you deepen your understanding and use of acceptance.

- Describe something that is causing you significant anxiety right now.

- What is it that you don't want to accept? Why is it hard to accept?

- What is this doing to the quality of your life?

- How are you dealing with it? (Avoidance? Safety behaviors?)

- If you accepted its presence in your life, what's the worst that could happen?

- How would you deal with it if that were to happen?

- What would change for you and your life if you accepted it? (You might think of both positive and negative changes, and that's okay.)

- Describe what your life might be like if the anxiety-provoking situation was still there but you accepted it and moved forward anyway.

TAKEAWAYS

- Unpleasant emotions are part of the human experience.

- Since avoidance is hardwired into the brain, it's important to be patient with yourself while you shift toward acceptance.

- Avoidance doesn't work. It keeps us trapped and prevents us from living our lives fully.

- A shift in focus from avoidance to acceptance is what breaks us out of the trap and moves us forward into our real lives.

- With acceptance, we no longer avoid with waiting for someday; instead, we acknowledge our anxieties and choose to live fully in the present moment.

- Mindfulness is the key that opens the door to acceptance.

- Mindfulness allows us to explore, invite, and be compassionate with anxiety and difficult emotions, which in turn reduces their power over us.

PHOBIAS & AVOIDANCE

YOUR WEEK

DAY 1

READ:
The Challenge and The Solution

EXERCISE:
Who's Driving Your
Avoidance Car? (Part One)

DAY 2

EXERCISE:
Who's Driving Your
Avoidance Car? (Part Two)

EXERCISE:
Take It Further to Make You
Stronger

DAY 3

EXERCISE:
Hypothesis Testing (Part One)

DAY 4

EXERCISE:
Hypothesis Testing (Part Two)

EXERCISE:
Consider Yourself a Scientist

DAY 5

EXERCISE:
Gradual Exposure (Part One)

DAY 6

EXERCISE:
Gradual Exposure (Part Two)

DAY 7

HOMEWORK

The Challenge

Avoidance is a major player in developing—and exacerbating—phobias. When we encounter something that makes us feel very fearful, our brain sends messages to our body to avoid that thing at all costs. We have a built-in aversion to things we perceive as potentially dangerous or harmful. This natural aversive reaction is mostly helpful, because it's designed to keep us alive and safe by avoiding real threats. If you're not a strong swimmer, for example, your fear of deep water means you'll take precautions and wear a life jacket. That's a healthy, rational response to a rational fear. The challenge to our mental health and well-being comes when our fear responses become irrational, and we start to fear and avoid things that pose no real threat.

Fear is a basic human reaction to danger or the unknown. However, when fear of a particular situation or thing reaches unhealthy levels, we call it a *phobia*. Phobias are the result of fear that has gotten out of hand and begins to take over our lives. This table shows the difference between fears and phobias:

Fear	Phobia
Limited: You really don't like riding your bike along a particularly busy, dangerous street.	**Generalized:** You're afraid that you'll be hit by a bus on that busy street. There are buses and other big vehicles on many streets. Even though you used to love it, you won't ride your bike anywhere because you're afraid of being hit by a bus or another large vehicle.
Waxes and wanes: Sometimes the traffic on that street isn't so bad, and when it's not, you're not too afraid to ride there.	**Persistent:** Your fear of riding in traffic never gets better and in fact is getting worse.
Level of fear matches the intensity of the situation: Riding on that street in heavy traffic causes fear to spike and brings sensations of panic, whereas you don't feel afraid to ride your bike elsewhere.	**Level of fear is out of proportion to the situation:** Being in the car on a slow street and seeing someone on a bike creates intense fear and panic as you imagine yourself in their position getting hit by a large vehicle.

Fear	Phobia
The feeling does not dominate your thoughts: You think of riding your bike on that street only when you have to do it.	**Thoughts about your phobia can become obsessive, and you think about it even when you're not experiencing the thing or situation you fear:** Every day you are full of dread because it might be that day that your car won't start and you'll have to use your bike to get to work.
Being confronted by the feared situation creates a physical and emotional reaction: The fight-or-flight response. To get to work today, you have to ride your bike, and you'll be on the busy street. Your heart pounds as you ride, you feel nauseated and dizzy, or you start to sweat, or you feel like you might cry. But once you are off that street, your physiological and psychological responses gradually calm back down.	**The natural fight-or-flight response is almost always heightened. This response is so easily activated that it starts to get in the way of your normal life:** Listening to the morning traffic report, you learned of an accident blocking a highway. If you had been biking there at that moment, you might have been killed. You have a panic attack, and you feel ill. You call in sick and stay home from work.
Fear is felt and experienced, but it doesn't restrict your life: While your fear is unpleasant, you don't need to avoid riding your bike altogether.	**Your excessive fear leads to avoidance and is very life-limiting:** You've given up riding, and you've dropped out of the riding group you belonged to. Your spouse is still in the group, and it's painful to see her go off on weekend rides. Your weekends now involve sitting in front of the television, alone. You can tell this phobia is affecting your physical and mental health, and it's taking its toll on your marriage.
You are aware of the fear and can take measures to deal with it: You add mirrors to your bike so you can see traffic approaching you from behind, mount daytime visibility head- and taillights, and wear a bright, high-visibility vest so drivers can see you.	**You are aware of the phobia and that it is excessive and irrational but can't do anything about it:** You know that it is irrational to be this afraid of riding your bike. You've ridden for fun and transportation from the time you were a kid until a few years ago when this excessive and irrational phobia developed seemingly out of the blue. Something must have started it, but you don't know what it was. You do know that it has taken over and nothing you do can reduce your fear. The only thing you can do is avoid your bike, but you hate it.

WHERE DO PHOBIAS COME FROM?

According to the American Psychiatric Association in the *Diagnostic and Statistical Manual of Mental Disorders, Fifth Edition,* or *DSM-5* (2013), phobias can develop at any age and have a variety of sources:

- Traumatic events (not necessarily violent; for example, being stuck in an elevator can be traumatic to some people).

- Observing others experience traumatic events.

- Information overload from constant media coverage of an event like a plane crash, shooting, fire, etc.

- Unexpected panic attack in a specific situation; the setting or circumstance where the panic attack took place will become the source of the phobia.

Online assessments can be your first step to identifying a specific phobia. However, these tests don't provide clinical diagnosis; instead they give you a broad stroke analysis. They can help you clarify some of your symptoms and give you pointers for reaching out to a doctor or therapist.

It's important to do an online test that's been created and vetted by certified mental health professionals. The Anxiety and Depression Association of America (ADAA) is one such trustworthy resource. ADAA offers the Screening for Specific Phobias, a free questionnaire that also checks for co-occurring anxiety and depression symptoms. You can find it on their website: https://adaa.org/living-with-anxiety/ask-and-learn/screenings/screening-specific-phobias.

People go to great lengths to avoid phobic reactions. Whether that means canceling plans, avoiding public places, or drastically restricting their daily activities, people in the grip of a phobia will use almost any strategy that allows them to avoid that scary phobic response of anxiety or even panic. A person who is afraid to fly might turn down a promotion—and the sizeable pay raise that comes with it—because the new position requires travel. Another might drive an extra hour every morning and again every evening just to avoid driving across a bridge. Yet another person might find it difficult to even leave their house, for fear of germs. If you examine your own fear patterns closely, you will probably find that your fears and phobias, while very uncomfortable and downright painful, aren't the real problem. The problem is your reaction, your repeated choice to *avoid* what you fear. It is this avoidance that gets in your way. This is true for everyone.

The Solution: Hypothesis Testing and Gradual Exposure

The chronic avoidance that accompanies phobias does two main things: First, it prevents growth by keeping you stuck in your fear; when you don't give yourself the chance to encounter what it is you fear, you neither learn about the fear nor how you really react to it. The only information you have is what you've made up in your head, and you have likely overestimated the threat your fear poses. Secondly, avoidance limits your life by restricting where you can go, what you can do, and the people you can see.

Fortunately, the solution to the problem of avoidance lies with you. This chapter will offer a combination of hypothesis testing and low-level exposure, and will explain how to use these practices in your daily life. Examining the true nature of your fears eventually allows you to adopt healthier, more realistic thoughts and beliefs about the things that cause you anxiety. When you look at the full picture of your behaviors and explore the reasons why you were avoiding specific situations, you equip yourself with the knowledge you need to make different choices in the future.

Phobias are typically treated with an individualized action plan that includes a few different treatment approaches. Phobic avoidance is stubborn and initially resistant to change, so a single treatment approach by itself sometimes isn't enough to manage these challenges. Combined, though, these strategies are quite effective. For dealing with phobias, the healing approaches include:

Cognitive therapy. With cognitive therapy, you delve deeper into your fears to tease out your underlying beliefs about them. We have used a few cognitive strategies already in this program. Close examination of your fearful thoughts readies you to replace them with healthier ones, which in turn frees you to take new actions.

Exposure therapy. This type of treatment targets your behavior. Here, you directly face your fears, intentionally putting yourself in contact with the scary thing you've been avoiding. The thought of doing this might be uncomfortable and anxiety provoking, but keep in mind that along the way you'll also be working on identifying irrational beliefs and developing healthier, more realistic ones.

Relaxation training and mindfulness. Confronting fears can sometimes exacerbate the fight-or-flight response, which is already active thanks to the phobia itself. Exposing yourself to something you fear releases adrenaline, cortisol, and other stress hormones, preparing your body to run the other way. The point of exposure therapy is to beat avoidance by staying with the fear despite discomfort and the powerful urge to avoid. This is possible with the help of relaxation and mindfulness techniques.

Who's Driving Your Avoidance Car?

Many of us know that our fears and phobias are irrational. We're completely aware that they prevent us from participating in the things we love with the people we care about. However, we can't stop our brains from being controlled by fear. The "flight" part of fight-or-flight screams at you to run. Even when you're well aware that avoidance will cause you to miss out on people or things you really value, you may still let fear make your decisions for you.

Fight-or-flight is an instinctive reaction to danger and fear. It hijacks functions of the brain and body to prepare you to either battle or retreat. There isn't much actual thought involved; it's an automatic physiological reaction driven by fears, phobias, and anxieties. That doesn't mean, however, that you're powerless to use your brain to think in fearful circumstances. In fact, the power of your thoughts can reduce your fear and avoidance reactions when you approach a scary situation.

Once again, it's helpful to know what, exactly, is driving your avoidance. Which specific beliefs and irrational fears are causing your urge to avoid certain people, places, or situations? Identifying these issues helps empower you to face them head-on.

WHO'S DRIVING YOUR AVOIDANCE CAR? (PART ONE)

1. List Your Fears. Make a list of fears that are interfering with your enjoyment of life. Write down at least three or four, but feel free to list as many as you want to. Each of us has more than one fear, and many people have a significant number of fears and phobias. Giving thoughtful consideration to all of the drivers of your avoidance car will help you take on one driver after another until you're the only one behind the wheel.

_____

_____

_____

_____

_____

2. What do you think will happen? Let's take a look at your theories that underlie your fears. Now that you have listed your fears, it's time to identify the beliefs behind them. Choose one of the fears on your list. Release your thoughts and expose them by getting them out of your head and onto paper.

This example will get you going:

3. Write down the fear you've selected from your list and how it's limiting your life.

I'm afraid of having to talk to a group of people.

4. What do you think will happen if you're in a group and you think you're going to have to talk?

It will be like I'm giving a speech to a massive group of people. I'll start to sweat and tremble, and my face will probably turn red. Everyone will stare and think I'm weird.

5. What do you think will happen if someone asks you a question or for your opinion?

I might not be able to talk, and they'll think I'm stupid. They'll laugh at me and then walk away, leaving me by myself. Or I might talk but say the wrong things. I might say something they don't want to hear.

6. What do you think will happen if you say the wrong thing or don't say anything at all?

I'll look ridiculous, and I'll be mortified. I might be so upset that I have an anxiety attack. Then

people will really laugh at me. My reputation will be ruined, and no one will like me.

7. Close your eyes and imagine yourself with your fear. Describe what you're picturing in your mind.

I'll get to my kid's soccer game, and parents will be standing around. They'll wave me over.

I'll be nervous, and I'll drop the lawn chair I'm carrying. It will be loud, and people will stare.

They'll laugh. I'll go over anyway, but I'll already be shaking. I feel dumb already. Someone will

make a negative comment about the coach and look at me. What will I say? I don't want to

bash the coach but I don't want to seem weird for not joining in. I will try to talk, but I won't

be able to because I'm having an anxiety attack. My son will see it and be ashamed. I won't be

able to go to his games ever again. I'll just stay at home. It's better that way.

Now it's your turn to explore your thoughts about one of your fears:

1. Write down the fear you've selected from your list and how it's limiting your life.

2. What do you think will happen if you have to go through with it?

3. What do you think will happen if you have to confront it and can't leave?

_____

_____

_____

4. How, exactly, will you be harmed in this situation?

_____

_____

_____

_____

5. Close your eyes and imagine yourself with your fear. Describe what you're picturing in your mind.

_____

_____

_____

_____

6. Finally, go back to the first line on which you wrote your fear. On a scale from 1 to 10, with 1 being very low and 10 being extremely high, how would you rate your level of anxiety caused by this fear? Write that number beside your written answer. Do the same for each of the proposed situations. Does your anxiety change in severity, or does it remain constant? There isn't a right or wrong answer. Simply observe your anxiety and whether it changes.

_____

_____

_____

DAY 2

WHO'S DRIVING YOUR AVOIDANCE CAR? (PART TWO)

Choose another fear from your list and repeat this process, getting to the depth of your thoughts about the fear.

1. Write down the fear you've selected from your list and how it's limiting your life.

_____

_____

_____

2. What do you think will happen if you have to go through with it?

_____

_____

_____

_____

3. What do you think will happen if you have to confront it and can't leave?

_____

_____

_____

_____

4. How, exactly, will you be harmed in this situation?

_____

_____

_____

_____

5. Close your eyes and imagine yourself with your fear. Describe what you're picturing in your mind.

_____

_____

_____

_____

_____

_____

_____

6. Now, return again to the first line on which you wrote your fear and rate your anxiety levels for the fear itself and for your thoughts about each situation using the 1 to 10 scale.

EXERCISE

TAKE IT FURTHER TO MAKE YOU STRONGER

Reflect on this experience of examining your thoughts about what would happen if you had to confront your fears. Did you notice anything about your thinking? How could you use your increased awareness about your thoughts to reduce both your fear and avoidance? What will it be like when you're back in the driver's seat of your life car?

Hypothesis Testing

You've identified some of your major thoughts and beliefs and have a better under-standing of what's driving your fear and avoidance. Now, it's time to take a look at some of these beliefs and rate their accuracy, or how realistic they are. This will be our first step in what scientists call "hypothesis testing."

Here's the process:

1. Choose a fearful thought, one that you identified in Who's Driving Your Avoidance Car? (Part One). Or explore a different fear and belief. You will write this down in the left side of the table on page 117. Also, using the same 1 to 10 scale that we've been practic-ing, write the level of anxiety that this causes you.

2. Read the thought you wrote in the left-hand column and ask yourself how likely it is that this will happen.

Questioning your thoughts in this way is a form of hypothesis testing. You have new ideas about your world, so you're no longer accepting your fear at face value. You're now questioning the reality of your fears. How do your fearful thoughts hold up against your questioning? Some thoughts might stubbornly resist change because we still insist on their accuracy. Other fearful, unrealistic thoughts will crumble under the weight of your questioning, your hypothesis testing. You're just testing out different ideas right now, which is a very important part of ending avoidance and moving past fears and phobias.

3. After you've questioned the belief you wrote in the left column, write a new, more realistic belief in the right column. Then, rate your anxiety on the 1 to 10 scale. Did it change? Why did you give it the number you did?

HYPOTHESIS TESTING (PART ONE)

Using the example to get you started, do some hypothesis testing. List a fearful thought, pause to question it, and write and rank a new belief. Do this for three beliefs that are contributing to fear and avoidance.

Fearful Thought	New, Reality-Based Thought
I'm afraid to eat in public. I worry that people will keep demanding that I eat. They'll insist that I eat something and stand there watching me until I do. Then I'll be forced to eat in front of others, and I'll be mortified. My anxiety level about being forced to eat in front of people is a 10.	I've never seen people actually force each other to eat. The chances of someone being so insistent and forceful about my eating is probably pretty slim. My anxiety level about being forced to eat is a 6. I mean, it could happen. But it probably won't. I'm still uncomfortable, but I can handle an anxiety level of 6. I'll stop by the party for 10 minutes and see what happens.

DAY 4

HYPOTHESIS TESTING (PART TWO)

Don't stop now! Today you're going to do a bit more hypothesis testing. Tackle three more beliefs the same way you did yesterday.

Fearful Thought	New, Reality-Based Thought
If I don't eat, someone will shove food into my mouth. I won't go to the party and risk that happening. My anxiety level about someone shoving food into my mouth is a 10.	I've never seen people shove food into each other's mouths. The chances of someone shoving food into my mouth are probably pretty slim. My anxiety level about someone shoving food into my mouth is a 6. I mean, it could happen. But it probably won't. I'm still uncomfortable, but I can handle an anxiety level of 6. I'll stop by the party for 10 minutes and see what happens.

EXERCISE

CONSIDER YOURSELF A SCIENTIST

 Examine your fears and avoidance as if they are hypotheses that need to be questioned and tested. Ask yourself: What other fearful beliefs are you harboring that are causing you to avoid parts of your life? Are they accurate and realistic? How can they be replaced? What effect do your hypotheses have on your anxiety? Reflect on these ideas as you continue to test your thoughts to see just how accurate—or inaccurate—they are.

Exposure

By now, you've identified your fears and avoidance behaviors. You've examined the fearful thoughts and theories that bolster your phobias and avoidance. You've begun to test your hypotheses by questioning your fears and related behaviors. Not only that, you're using this new information to rewrite your hypotheses based on the information you've discovered about what actually happens when you are in a scary situation. Now, it's time to gradually begin to face your fears in the world and stop avoiding things that are propelling your anxiety.

EXERCISE

GRADUAL EXPOSURE (PART ONE)

Choose one fear to confront. With this type of exposure, it's important to start with something small—that's the *gradual* part. It should be something that actually causes anxiety and is restricting your life, but it shouldn't be so huge that it's overwhelming to handle. Success comes from starting small and working your way toward bigger things.

1. What have you been avoiding due to fear or significant discomfort?

_____

_____

_____

2. On a scale from 1 to 10, what is your anxiety level when you think of this fear? _____

3. What is one thing you can do to put yourself closer to your fear?

_____

_____

_____

4. On a scale from 1 to 10, what is your anxiety level when you make a plan that pushes you closer to your fear? _____

Do that thing today. Whether it is a visualization activity or something active, take as much time as you need to confront your fear for the first time.

5. Describe what it was like to be near your fear in any way and to stay with it rather than avoid it. How did your anxiety respond to doing this exposure exercise?

_____

_____

_____

_____

_____

_____

_____

_____

_____

_____

_____

_____

_____

_____

_____

_____

EXERCISE

GRADUAL EXPOSURE (PART TWO)

You're behind the wheel, and you're driving forward, toward a life without limits! Yesterday you began gradual exposure. Today you'll repeat the exercise and continue your forward momentum.

1. Choose another small fear to confront. What have you been avoiding due to fear or significant discomfort?

---

2. On a scale from 1 to 10, what is your anxiety level when you think of your fear?

---

3. What is one thing you can do to move closer to your fear?

---

4. On a scale from 1 to 10, what is your anxiety level when you think about doing the thing that moves you closer to your fear?

Do that one thing today. Whether it's a visualization activity, or confronting your feared situation or thing in real life, take the first step today.

5. Describe what it was like to be near your fear in any way and to stay with it rather than avoid it. How did your anxiety respond to doing this? Did it spike? Did it stay about the same? How long did your anxiety last?

Homework

In order to get effective results, exposure should be done regularly and consistently. Ideally, each day you'll take a small step closer to conquering the thing or situation you fear.

Create a daily plan for one of your phobic or feared objects. Each day, do a bit more to face it. Your goal is to loosen fear's grip by confronting it, freeing yourself to live fully instead of avoiding your life out of fear. For example, these are some activities that you could do if you are a parent who is afraid to talk in groups:

- Go to a coffee shop with a close friend or relative and talk to each other as if you were at home.

- Bring your friend or relative with you to your kid's soccer game and notice how comfortable you feel chatting with just them on the sidelines.

- Have your friend or relative come with you to the next game, and this time, mingle with the other groups of parents. Ask your friend to introduce you to the others.

Now that you're acquainted with the other parents, try going to the next game by yourself. Greet the group of parents and wait until you feel comfortable enough to join in the conversation.

TAKEAWAYS

- The fight-or-flight response can protect us, but it gets out of hand when fear becomes excessive and causes us to avoid basic necessities in our lives.

- Phobias are the result of fear that has reached unhealthy, life-disrupting levels of avoidance.

- Avoidance is a behavior born out of fear and the desire to protect ourselves from unpleasant thoughts, emotions, and situations.

- You can overcome fears, phobias, and avoidance so you can move forward and live life fully despite feeling afraid.

- Ways to reduce fears, phobias, and avoidance include cognitive therapy (working on your beliefs and hypotheses about the things you fear), exposure therapy (moving *toward* the things you fear—the opposite of avoidance), and relaxation training and mindfulness.

WEEK SEVEN

BODY AWARENESS

YOUR WEEK

DAY 1

READ:
The Challenge and The Solution

EXERCISE:
Lovingkindness Body Meditation
(5 minutes)

EXERCISE:
Mindful Body Scan (5 minutes)

DAY 2

EXERCISE:
Mindful Body Scan (10 minutes)

EXERCISE:
Thinking About Your
Body Scans

DAY 3

EXERCISE:
Outdoor Mindfulness Walking
Meditation (15 minutes)

DAY 4

EXERCISE:
Indoor Mindfulness Walking
Meditation (15 minutes)

EXERCISE:
Reflect on Your Experience

DAY 5

EXERCISE:
Mindful Movement in the Real
World (10 minutes)

DAY 6

EXERCISE:
Mindful Movement in an
Imagined World (10 minutes)

EXERCISE:
Your Mindful Movement
Experience

DAY 7

HOMEWORK

The Challenge

As we've learned, anxiety is very much a product of our *thoughts*. Most researchers and therapists now believe that it's really not a specific situation or external issue that creates anxious feelings; instead it's our exaggerated, irrational *thoughts* about the situation that cause us difficulties. Just remembering that your thoughts aren't always true is tricky enough. But anxiety also triggers body cues that reinforce the idea that our anxiety is rooted in reality: when you're sweating, and your heart is racing, and you have trouble catching your breath, your body is telling you that the threat is not exaggerated—it's real.

Here's a scenario to illustrate what I mean. Imagine that you've worked all day on an elaborate four-course meal for your boss and his wife who are coming over for dinner. An hour before they are supposed to arrive, your boss calls to cancel. His wife hasn't been feeling well all day, and now she has a fever. He is very sorry and hopes you'll forgive them and reschedule. While you might feel a little frustrated that you'd spent so much time cooking that day, nothing really bad will happen as a result of the cancellation.

But your bodily sensations may tell you a different story. When you hang up the phone, a flash of heat travels up your spine. Your heart starts pounding; suddenly, you start to wonder if your boss is lying. Your mind starts to desperately scan for instances when you've performed poorly at work. Is that why your boss canceled? Because he thinks you're a loser? It's only 7 p.m., but all of a sudden, you feel tired, like you've been up all night long. If anxiety hadn't taken over your thoughts and your bodily responses, you might be disappointed, but you wouldn't blame yourself or worry that your boss didn't like you.

Anxiety almost always shows up in the body and makes our irrational responses seem that much more true to us. Physical symptoms of anxiety can include one or more of the following:

- Headaches
- Lightheadedness/dizziness
- Blurred vision
- Coughing
- Difficulty breathing/shortness of breath
- Pounding heart
- Chest pain
- Nausea/vomiting
- Acid reflux
- Stomach discomfort
- Diarrhea and/or constipation (irritable bowel syndrome)
- Frequent urination
- Sweating
- Muscle tension, twitches, pain
- Joint pain
- Shaking
- Difficulty getting or staying asleep/insomnia

Anxiety symptoms exhibit themselves differently in everyone, and our anxiety responses are just as unique as our thoughts. You might experience flares of acid reflux while someone else might be plagued by joint pain. Those are just two examples of physical symptoms anxiety can cause.

THE MIND-BODY CONNECTION

Psychology, holistic traditions, and alternative medicine teach us the importance of the "mind-body connection." The mind and body are part of the same system and are already in sync with each other. Think for a moment about how your body feels when your thoughts and emotions are anxious and upset. Brainstorm situations that make you anxious, and note how you feel physically when you're in those situations. Two examples help you start.

Anxieties: Worries, Ruminations, Fears/Phobias, Emotions	Bodily Sensation(s)
I'm dreading the company picnic, because I'll look like a fool during the games and people will make fun of me behind my back.	Loss of appetite, headache.
I'm afraid of elevators, but I have to go all the way up to the 18th floor. I don't think I can go up that many flights of stairs and still make my appointment on time. I don't know what to do.	Pounding heart, difficulty breathing, sweating, pressure of tears behind the eyes.

Another way the mind-body connection factors in here has to do with overall wellness. Recognizing the connection between our anxiety and our physical well-being is an essential step in learning to manage our anxiety in healthy ways and prevent a worsening of symptoms. You can do all this by learning how to focus on the sensations in your body.

The Solution: Cultivate Body Awareness

Turning inward and paying purposeful attention to the signals your body is sending you is a powerful mindfulness exercise. It connects the mind and body in a way that allows you to communicate with yourself. Cultivating body awareness is beneficial in many ways:

- Quiets your mind so you can listen to your body.

- Helps you learn about your body's unique response to stress and anxiety.

- Shows you where to focus your breathing and relaxation efforts, including, but not limited to, tensing and releasing, gently massaging the area with your fingertips, using aromatherapy by rubbing a scented lotion or cream into the spot, and breathing into a stressed area.

- Cultivates lovingkindness for yourself and your body, as you gently notice and acknowledge your body's cues.

Here's an example of how the lovingkindness meditation from week five can be adapted to a body awareness and compassion exercise.

EXERCISE

LOVINGKINDNESS BODY MEDITATION (5 MINUTES)

1. Get comfortable by sitting or lying down.

2. Set your timer for 5 minutes.

3. Breathe in slowly, through your nose. Hear the air moving into your body.

4. Pause briefly and feel your body hold the air. Feel the sensation in your lungs, your diaphragm, your entire chest cavity.

5. Exhale slowly through your mouth, feeling the air pass across your lips as your belly relaxes. Feel your chest cavity return to its original size. Feel your shoulders relax and descend back toward your core.

6. Continue to breathe deeply for several breaths, feeling your body react to the air coming in and going out.

7. Say the following statements aloud as you contemplate the words:

- May I notice how my body feels, from the big things down to the tiniest sensations in my toes and fingertips.

- May I pause when I "hear" a part of my body communicating with me and stay with that body part, giving it my undivided attention and compassion.

- May I ask my lungs (or other area) what is making them feel this way and what would help them feel better.

- May I live my day compassionately for my lungs (or other area), intentionally taking care of their needs by taking breaks, practicing stress relief, deep breathing, and taking short walks.

You can do a lovingkindness exercise for your body immediately following any of the mindfulness exercises in this chapter. But you can do these body-focused mindfulness exercises anytime; perhaps first thing in the morning, or just before you go to sleep.

Cultivating body awareness can help you start reducing your physical symptoms of anxiety. Now, let's turn to more mindfulness exercises designed for that purpose.

Body Scan

EXERCISE
MINDFUL BODY SCAN (5 MINUTES)

A body scan is a way of getting in touch with what's physically going on inside of you, from head to toe. It prompts you to identify any areas of tension, pain, or discomfort. Remember, observe these sensations, but don't judge them. Your body simply feels the way it feels. There are no "bad" or "good" sensations. Things just *are*. When you sense something negative or uncomfortable, keep your attention there, breathing deeply as you maintain your focus on the area in the spirit of acceptance and compassion. Try it now:

1. Get comfortable by sitting or lying down.

2. Set your timer for 5 minutes.

3. Breathe in slowly, through your nose. Hear the air moving into your body.

4. Pause briefly and feel your body hold the air.

5. Exhale slowly through your mouth, feeling the air pass across your lips as your belly relaxes.

6. Continue to breathe deeply for several breaths, feeling your body react to the air coming in and going out.

7. Start your attention at your feet. Wiggle your toes, then flex them. Roll your ankles. Imagine the blood flowing to and through your feet, giving them oxygen and other nourishment.

8. Move your attention up to your lower legs. Squeeze your calves, hold for a few counts, and then release. Imagine blood delivering nutrients throughout your entire lower legs.

9. Progress to your knees and upper legs. Squeeze and release your knees, your thigh muscles, your buttocks. Picture your blood coursing through this entire area, contributing to health.

10. Starting at your navel and moving up to the top of your torso, scan your abdominal area. Pause at your chest and breathe into your heart, your lungs. Tense and relax the muscles in this area.

11. Turn your attention to your lower back, then middle back, then upper back. What do you feel?

12. Pay attention to your shoulders. Move them slightly before scanning your upper arms. Tense the muscles of your upper arm, and let go.

13. Continue scanning past your elbow, down your lower arms, over your wrists, and into your hands. Flex your fingers and release. Rotate your wrists.

14. Move to your neck, jaw, cheek muscles, and forehead. Notice and breathe.

15. Finally, scan your head, ending at the crown of your head. Feel your energy gathering there, flowing down your body to your toes and back up to the top of your head.

16. Gently open your eyes, flex your fingers and toes, and smile.

EXERCISE

MINDFUL BODY SCAN (10 MINUTES)

Repeat the mindful body scan, only this time, double the length of time you spend on it. Scan more slowly, and stay with each area longer than you did the first time around. Staying with the areas of discomfort rather than avoiding them is what ultimately helps with the physical symptoms of anxiety because you become aware of what you need to do to heal.

1. Set your timer for 10 minutes.

2. Get comfortable by sitting or lying down.

3. Breathe in slowly, through your nose. Hear the air moving into your body.

4. Pause briefly and feel your body hold the air.

5. Exhale slowly through your mouth, feeling the air pass across your lips as your belly relaxes.

6. Continue to breathe deeply for several breaths, feeling your body react to the air coming in and going out.

7. Begin at your feet. Wiggle your toes, then flex them. Roll your ankles. Imagine the blood flowing to and through your feet, giving them oxygen and other nourishment.

8. Move your attention up to your lower legs. Squeeze your calves, hold for a few counts, and then release. Imagine blood delivering nutrients throughout your entire lower legs.

9. Progress to your knees and upper legs. Squeeze and release your knees, your thigh muscles, your buttocks. Picture your blood coursing through this entire area, contributing to health.

10. Starting at your navel and moving up to the top of your torso, scan your abdominal area. Pause at your chest and breathe into your heart, your lungs. Tense and relax the muscles in this area.

11. Turn your attention to your lower back, then middle back, then upper back. What do you feel?

12. Pay attention to your shoulders. Move them slightly before scanning your upper arms. Tense the muscles of your upper arm and let go.

13. Continue scanning past your elbow, down your lower arms, over your wrists, and into your hands. Flex your fingers and release. Rotate your wrists.

14. Move to your neck, jaw, cheek muscles, and forehead. Notice and breathe.

15. Finally, scan your head, ending at the crown of your head. Feel your energy gathering there, flowing down your body to your toes and back up to the top of your head.

16. Gently open your eyes, flex your fingers and toes, and smile.

EXERCISE

THINKING ABOUT YOUR BODY SCANS

What insights about your body has the mindfulness body scan brought to your attention? What actions can you take to begin to soothe any uncomfortable areas in your body? Think of little things you can do every single day, and write them here:

Walking Meditation

Have you ever been on your way somewhere when all of a sudden you realized that you were at your destination but you had no idea how you got there? You have no memory of the walk, drive, or metro ride that brought you from point A to point B. This is a common experience, and it usually happens because we put ourselves on autopilot and think of other things. In other words, our minds are everywhere other than on what we're doing in the moment. On autopilot, we're not being mindful of our present moment, and we quickly lose track of ourselves.

Anxiety can cause us to switch over to autopilot, too. When our minds are busy ruminating over anxious thoughts, we become tangled up in worries, fears, and our plans to avoid these worries and fears. We're so busy with our anxiety that we miss out on a lot of our lives. One very effective, and calming, way to slow down and turn our thoughts away from anxious ruminations is to ground ourselves in what is happening in the here and now, around us and within us. When we use mindfulness to connect our bodies and our surroundings, we experience what is really happening *right now*.

Like the other meditations in this book, walking meditations are grounding exercises you can do anywhere, at any time. As you do them, you'll learn how to experience the beauty of life between each starting and stopping point. Mindfulness and meditation expert Jon Kabat-Zinn offers us important insights about walking meditation:

- The goal isn't to arrive somewhere but instead is to move and to be with each step.

- Walking meditations let us participate in our body's experiences in a different way than stationary meditations.

- As with all mindfulness meditations, when the mind wanders, observe it and gently bring it back to your experience of walking.

- You can walk at any speed you wish; there is no right or wrong way to walk.

- Place your hands where they are comfortable for you. Let them hang at your sides, clasp them behind you or in front of you, or place them in your pockets. There isn't a right or a wrong way to keep your arms and hands. Just let them be and increase your awareness of them as part of your mindful walk.

- Keep your mind and body together, in harmony, focused on the moment.

- Keep these tips in mind as you engage in these walking meditation exercises.

EXERCISE

OUTDOOR MINDFULNESS WALKING MEDITATION (15 MINUTES)

The world is at your feet for this walking meditation. You can step into your backyard and walk, you can walk around your block, you can walk in a park, on a path, on a busy city street, or on a nature trail. Choose what brings you joy. Once you've selected your spot, follow these directions for a peaceful walking mindfulness meditation:

1. Set your timer for 15 minutes.

2. Close your eyes and inhale slowly and deeply. Notice the feel of the fresh air as it enters and leaves your body. Take note of any smells. Feel the temperature and wind speed.

3. Stand with your feet firmly planted on the ground. Starting with your feet, do a body scan to increase your awareness of your entire body.

4. Slowly lift one foot, paying purposeful attention to the movement of your leg, the bend in your knee. Feel your foot suspended above the ground.

5. Place that same foot in front of you. Feel your knee straighten, your leg descend, and your heel touch the ground followed by the ball of your foot and your toes.

6. Repeat this rhythm of forward movement until your timer sounds. If you'd like to continue, by all means do.

EXERCISE

INDOOR MINDFULNESS WALKING MEDITATION (15 MINUTES)

Walking meditations can be done indoors just as well as outdoors. When you walk inside, you can remove your shoes and socks so your feet can fully feel the bare floor. Choose an area such as a hallway, stairs, or path from room to room. When you reach the end of your path, turn around and walk back in the other direction.

1. Set your timer for 15 minutes.

2. Remove your shoes and socks. Close your eyes and inhale slowly and deeply. Notice the feel of the fresh air as it enters and leaves your body. Take note of any smells and the temperature of the indoor air.

3. Stand with your feet firmly planted on the ground. Starting with your feet, do a body scan to increase your awareness of your entire body.

4. Slowly lift one foot, paying purposeful attention to the movement of your leg, the bend in your knee. Feel your foot suspended above the floor.

5. Place that same foot in front of you. Feel your knee straighten, your leg descend, and your heel touch the floor followed by the ball of your foot and your toes.

6. Repeat this rhythm of forward movement until your timer sounds. If you'd like to continue, by all means do.

REFLECT ON YOUR EXPERIENCE

Walking mediations bring our attention back to the present moment. They help us stop blindly rushing through life, letting anxiety guide us, and missing out on things that are important to us. Reflect on and write down some of the impressions that came to you during these walking mindfulness meditations. What did you notice about your body? What were your thoughts like during the experience? How easy was it to return your thoughts to the moment when they wandered? How could this help you manage anxiety in your daily life?

Mindful Movement

When we move gently and purposefully and feel the experience of our bodies moving, we calm our thoughts, focus our attention, root ourselves in the present moment, and reduce anxieties. Yoga and tai chi are examples of formal mindful movement practices. In the first mindful movement exercise, you'll pay attention to the actual space around you, and in the second, you'll move in an imagined scenario.

EXERCISE

MINDFUL MOVEMENT IN THE REAL WORLD (10 MINUTES)

1. Set your timer for 10 minutes. Turn on some enjoyable music if you'd like, or let the room stay silent.

2. Remove your shoes and socks. Close your eyes and inhale slowly and deeply. Notice the feel of the fresh air as it enters and leaves your body. Feel your body expand with each inhale and return to normal with each exhale.

3. Tuck your chin in to your chest. Feel the muscles react. Now move your neck so your head is back and you are looking up at the ceiling. Feel your muscles react. Roll your head gently from side to side.

4. Roll your shoulders up and back, and wiggle your arms. Move your legs and feet.

5. Begin to move about. You can walk, dance, move in place, do yoga poses, raise and lower your arms, bend your knees—simply move. Notice how the movement feels throughout your body.

6. Switch your attention back and forth between your bodily sensations and the space around you. What do you see? Hear? Smell? Feel? Incorporate touch into your movements, and note textures.

7. Continue to move and be present with your inner world and your outer space until the timer sounds.

DAY 6

MINDFUL MOVEMENT IN AN IMAGINED WORLD (10 MINUTES)

Today, you'll repeat the mindful movement exercise, only this time, you'll visualize a different space. There is no limit to what you can visualize. Use the imagery in this exercise, or choose a place meaningful to you, such as a favorite outdoor spot like a hiking trail, park, or your backyard, or perhaps someone else's home where you have fond memories.

1. Set your timer for 10 minutes. Turn on some enjoyable music if you'd like, or let the room be silent.

2. Remove your shoes and socks. Close your eyes and inhale slowly and deeply. Notice the feel of the fresh air as it enters and leaves your body. Feel your body expand with each inhale and return to normal with each exhale.

3. With eyes still closed, imagine a beautiful mountain valley. You're standing in a flowering meadow on a warm, sunny day. Butterflies flutter. A brook bubbles nearby. It is here that you will move mindfully. Hold the image in your mind, and picture yourself moving your body here.

4. Tuck your chin in to your chest. Feel the muscles react. Now move your neck so your head is back and you are looking up at the ceiling. Feel your muscles react. Roll your head gently from side to side.

5. Roll your shoulders up and back, and wiggle your arms. Stretch them wide, and feel butterflies land on them. Move your legs and feet. Let your toes play with the flowers.

6. Begin to move about. You can walk, dance, move in place, do yoga poses, raise and lower your arms, bend your knees—simply move. Notice how the movement feels throughout your body. Bend and pick a flower. How does it smell? Walk to the brook and place the flower in the water. Watch it drift away on the current. Step into the brook. How cold is it? How does the water feel as it rushes around your ankles? Are there little fish swimming around your feet? Reach down and grab a handful of sand. Roll it around in your hands, and hear it splash back into the water.

7. Switch your attention back and forth between your bodily sensations and the meadow. What do you see? Hear? Smell? Feel? What sensations do you notice in your body?

8. Continue to move and be present with your inner world and your surroundings until the timer sounds.

EXERCISE

YOUR MINDFUL MOVEMENT EXPERIENCE

Reflect on what these two movement exercises were like. How did tuning in to your movements affect your anxiety? When could you use movement and mindfulness to reduce anxious thoughts and the physical symptoms that come with them? What was the difference for you between mindful movement in the real world versus mindful movement in a visualized scenario?

_____

_____

_____

_____

_____

_____

_____

_____

_____

_____

_____

_____

DAY 7

Homework

Continue to use the body awareness exercises in order to tune in to your body. Eventually, you'll be able to notice where in your body your worries, fears, and anxieties have settled. From there, you can put these uncomfortable spots and sensations to work for you. They'll act as alerts and tell you to when you need to pause, breathe deeply, and be mindful of how you are doing in the moment.

Copy these questions into your notebook. Reflect on them now and return to them again and again as you practice mindfulness to connect your brain and body and reduce anxiety:

- How does your body respond to anxiety? Some possible symptoms are headache, digestive trouble (acid reflex, nausea, vomiting, diarrhea, constipation, etc.), muscle aches, joint pain, or any other feelings of pain or discomfort in times of stress, worry, or fear.

- What are your thoughts like when you're feeling these physical symptoms?

- What's going on in your life?

- How can you use one of the three mindfulness exercises you learned this week to improve your thoughts and physical sensations?

TAKEAWAYS

- Just as there's a link between our thoughts and our anxiety, there is a link between our body and our anxiety.

- Even though we don't always recognize it, anxiety shows up somewhere in the body.

- Turning inward to pay attention to the body is a powerful mindfulness exercise.

- Mindful body awareness is an important part of reducing anxiety.

- Lovingkindness meditation and body awareness can be directed toward sensations in the body to release anxiety and replace it with self-compassion.

PANIC ATTACKS

WEEK 8

YOUR WEEK

DAY 1

READ:
The Challenge and The Solution

EXERCISE:
The Panic within Me

EXERCISE:
Reflection

DAY 2

EXERCISE:
My Thoughts Matter

EXERCISE:
Awareness and Compassionate Thoughts

DAY 3

COMPLETE:
Warm-Up

EXERCISE:
Interoceptive Exposure (Part One)

EXERCISE:
Turning Inward

DAY 4

EXERCISE:
Interoceptive Exposure (Part Two)

EXERCISE:
Facing Down Obstacles

DAY 5

EXERCISE:
A Serene Mountain Meadow (15 minutes)

DAY 6

EXERCISE:
A Personal Space Just for You (15 minutes)

EXERCISE:
Reflection

DAY 7

HOMEWORK

The Challenge

Panic attacks are aptly named: we experience them as attacks on our very being, and when they are happening, we feel completely gripped, nearly paralyzed, by anxiety, fear, and panic. People can also experience intense physical symptoms—like a pounding heart, tremors, sweating, coughing, and visual and auditory distortions—because sometimes our anxiety response gets so overactivated that they cause physiological symptoms. It's like anxiety hijacks our body and sticks a metal object into our circuitry, temporarily shorting out our system. As with an electrical short circuit, there's a systemwide spark of energy (the brain's fight-or-flight response) and the system (our thoughts, emotions, behaviors, and physical symptoms) temporarily stops functioning correctly.

Panic attacks are the sudden onset of intense physical symptoms of anxiety. This can happen when someone encounters a feared object or situation. However, you can also have a panic attack seemingly out of nowhere. These attacks are felt from head to toe, both in the physical body and also cognitively in racing, panicky thoughts. This chart shows just how and where we can feel this overpowering effect of anxiety during a panic attack:

Our Physical Body	Emotional Effects	Our Thoughts	Effects on Our Behavior
Pounding heart	Fear, terror	I'm dying	Avoidance of situations that might cause another panic attack
Rapid pulse	Strong desire to escape (the "flight" response)	I'm going crazy	Withdrawal from public places
Fast, shallow breathing	Embarrassment over what other people might think	I'm having a heart attack	Increasing isolation from people, places, etc.
Difficulty getting enough air	Worry about impending doom	I'm losing control	Hyperventilating; Fleeing from where you are

Our Physical Body	Emotional Effects	Our Thoughts	Effects on Our Behavior
Numbness and/or tingling anywhere in the body	Depression	What if it happens again?	Repeated searches for health conditions; trips to the doctor or ER
Sweating and/or chills	Helplessness	Hyperfocus on physical symptoms and emotions	Lifestyle changes because of health concerns
Trembling, shaking	Hopelessness	Wondering what is real (derealization)	Quitting jobs or losing jobs due to absenteeism
Blurred vision	Generalized anxiety and worry	Wondering if you are real (depersonalization)	Lifestyle changes due to financial restrictions (loss of work time, medical bills)
Sensory distortions (things seem bright, loud, appear different)	Social anxiety (fear of being observed having a panic attack and judged negatively)	I shouldn't be like this	Lifestyle changes because of financial problems (medical bills, loss of employment)
Dizziness, lightheadedness	Shame	Other people are better than me	Cessation of activities that used to bring pleasure, stress relief, and anxiety reduction
Nausea, abdominal discomfort	Decreasing self-confidence (a believer in yourself as a worthy person)	I am useless	Developing and increasingly sedentary lifestyle
Choking, coughing	Decreasing self-efficacy (the belief in your ability to accomplish things)	I am a terrible partner/parent/ friend/person	Dropping out of school

Not every person who experiences panic attacks has every one of these symptoms. But the more severe the panic attack, the more symptoms you'll likely experience. Most of these symptoms peak within about 10 minutes and then begin to recede, but others can linger and continue to feel distressing after the actual panic attack has subsided.

Panic attacks are frightening and can be both physically and psychologically distressing. While a panic attack can definitely make you feel helpless and at the mercy of your powerful symptoms, the truth is you're *not* powerless in those moments. Using a combination of the strategies you've explored over the course of this program, you can learn to take back some control of your feelings and responses, even when you're feeling the intense emotions and racing thoughts of panic.

PANIC ATTACK OR ANXIETY ATTACK?

People often use the terms *panic attack* and *anxiety attack* interchangeably. *Anxiety attack* is also used to describe the sudden onset of the physical, emotional, and cognitive symptoms of gripping anxiety. This can be confusing. Are they the same thing? The answer is twofold: yes and no.

Both panic and anxiety attacks can feel physically and psychologically overwhelming, which is why they're used interchangeably. There is, however, a technical difference between the two. Panic attacks are part of a disorder in their own right; they are one of the primary features of panic disorder. The other feature of panic disorder is the fear of having another panic attack.

Anxiety attacks, on the other hand, aren't officially part of an anxiety disorder. That said, they can indeed be a symptom of any anxiety disorder, and even of anxiety that isn't a diagnosable disorder. *Anxiety attack* is a lay term that describes the symptoms listed in the chart. They happen as a result of generalized worry, social anxiety, fears, and phobias. They have a direct cause other than the fear of having a panic attack.

Whether your attacks happen in the context of panic disorder or as a result of anxious thoughts, emotions, and behaviors, they're miserable—and they're treatable.

The Solution: Awareness, Compassion & Acceptance

Awareness, acceptance, and self-compassion are very powerful mindfulness concepts that can be your lifeline in a panic attack. You've been cultivating awareness of yourself, your life, and the present moment since the very first week of this program. Self-compassion is a skill cultivated by lovingkindness practice, which can help alleviate the pressure of negative thoughts and worries. And with acceptance, you can learn to be present in your life and live it fully, even when anxiety and panic show up.

Let's take a deeper look into what these concepts mean:

Awareness: One of the scariest thing about panic attacks is that they can seem to come out of nowhere. However, self-awareness can help you prevent catastrophic thinking or the physical signs of anxiety from escalating into panic. When you tune in intentionally to your body and mind, you will notice subtle signals that could warn of a pending panic attack. Are your muscles tense, for example? Does your chest feel tight? Where are your thoughts and emotions? Just as you notice bubbles rising in a pot and hear a sizzling sound just before a pot of water boils over, you can observe changes in your mind and body that alert you to rising anxiety. When you mindfully observe the changes within, rather than reacting to them, you can turn down the heat before anxiety and panic boil over.

Self-compassion: Just as you used compassion to soothe difficult emotions in week five, you can also use self-compassion to quiet your racing, agitated thoughts during a panic attack. Panic attacks are overwhelming and make you feel out of control. When panic strikes, people often worry that others are watching and judging them—thinking that they're freaks or acting crazy. These self-judgments lead to embarrassment and shame, which exacerbate the anxiety they're already feeling. Self-compassion reminds us that we're not freaks or crazy people—we're simply experiencing a panic attack and having a pretty normal response to some pretty scary symptoms. Panic is the result of our fight-or-flight response going haywire—it's not a sign of weakness or a personal failure. Practicing self-compassion in these moments helps you let go of the embarrassment and shame that aren't rooted in reality—and can even make your panic symptoms worse.

Acceptance: Through acceptance, you will be able to stop struggling, fighting, and avoiding the presence of your anxiety and panic, and open up space to move forward with them as a part of your overall life experience. Instead of berating yourself for having anxious thoughts and feelings, you can simply acknowledge their presence, then move on to the much more rewarding work of deciding how to move your life forward in a positive direction.

What does each of these three concepts mean for *you* and your experiences with anxiety? Take a moment to reflect on these key ideas.

	Awareness	Compassion	Acceptance
What does this mindfulness concept mean to you personally?			
What are some challenges of using this principle to increase mindfulness and decrease anxiety?			
What positive changes will happen in your life when you use this principle despite the challenges?			

Panic Attack Worksheets

The following exercises involve two different worksheets, to be done on two consecutive days.

On the first day, you'll begin to increase your awareness of how you experience panic attacks in your body. Panic shows up differently for different people, and this exercise helps pinpoint what your individual experience is like. On the second day, you'll explore the important connection between your physical response to panic attacks and the thoughts that accompany them. Mind and body are tightly intertwined and understanding this powerful dynamic can help reduce panic and anxiety in the moment.

EXERCISE

THE PANIC WITHIN ME

This checklist indicates areas in the body where panic attacks may be felt. Check the box beside each physical area where you experience discomfort during a panic attack.

☐ Top of your head	☐ Upper back	☐ Digestive tract
☐ Face	☐ Lower back	(intestines/bowels)
☐ Ears	☐ Kidneys	☐ Thighs
☐ Jaw	☐ Abdominal muscles	☐ Calves
☐ Neck	☐ Digestive tract	☐ Ankles
☐ Shoulders	(esophagus/	☐ Feet/toes
☐ Arms	acid reflux)	☐ Sweating
☐ Hands/fingers	☐ Digestive tract	☐ Trembling/tremors
☐ Chest (lungs)	(stomach)	☐ Other
☐ Chest (heart)		

1. On a scale from 1 to 10, with 1 representing minimal distress and 10 representing extreme distress, rate each physical effect of your panic attacks. Think carefully, as it might be tempting to assign everything a 10. That's because panic attacks are so intense and feel so awful that it seems like all of your physical responses are equally strong. Usually, though, that's not the case. When you become aware of your body's reaction and the intensity of each effect, you can focus on those areas with mindful acceptance, compassion, and relaxation.

Physical symptom	Rating

2. Place a ✓ beside the physical sensations that you rated an 8 or above. These are the areas on which to focus your mindful attention during and immediately following a panic attack. (You'll learn tools to help with this in the following exercises.)

3. Focusing on the positive is just as important as examining your problem areas. That's why you should now go back and put a ☺ beside those physical sensations you rated 5 or below. It can be hard to remember in the moment, but you are *not* fully consumed by anxiety and panic! That's a good sign.

EXERCISE
REFLECTION

In your journal, reflect on your increasing awareness of your bodily sensations during a panic attack. As you completed the worksheet, did anything surprise you? How difficult was it to rate the intensity of a panic attack's effect on your physical body? What personal meaning did you gain from doing this exercise? How will you use your new insights and meaning going forward?

EXERCISE

MY THOUGHTS MATTER

You've learned how the mind and body are connected. Where one goes, the other follows. If the mind is full of catastrophic thoughts, the body feels it in the form of racing heart, headaches, and general physical discomfort. The mind-body relationship works both ways: if the body is tense, in pain, or otherwise feeling sensations associated with anxiety, the mind interprets these sensations with anxious thoughts. This is why mindfulness works so well for reducing anxiety and panic. Just as the mind and body make up the motherboard for our anxiety, they also steer us toward confidence and calmness.

Yesterday you completed The Panic Within Me worksheet, focused on the physical signs of panic attacks. Today, you'll turn your attention to the thoughts that occur in tandem with your physical symptoms during a panic attack. When you increase your awareness of how catastrophic thinking and physical reactions mirror each other, you can use one to soothe the other, which will, in turn, deescalate both the thoughts and physical sensations associated with panic.

To begin, let's return to yesterday's worksheet. You checked the bodily responses that were the most troublesome to you. Now, list them in the left column. Complete the chart for each of the physical responses. Use the example to get started.

Panic Effects in the Body	THOUGHTS ABOUT THE EFFECTS	ADDITIONAL BODY SENSATIONS THAT ARISE OR INCREASE
Nausea	I'm going to be sick. I'm not near a bathroom, and people are around. I'm going to vomit all over in front of them and make a scene. They'll think I'm gross, and they'll call me names and make fun of me. I'll never be able to show my face here again.	It's harder to breathe. I can't get enough air. I'm going to vomit and then faint in it.

I will vomit: 5 I will faint: 5 I will do both: 3 People will make fun of me and call me names: 2 I'll never be able to show my face here again: 2	My stomach is queasy and nauseous. My body reacts this way during panic attacks, and I haven't vomited or fainted before. While it wouldn't be ideal to vomit or faint while panicking in public, it's doubtful that I'd be shamed. This reaction is my body's reaction to anxiety, nothing more and nothing less. May my thoughts and physical responses lighten as I practice mindful awareness, compassion, and acceptance.

AWARENESS AND COMPASSIONATE THOUGHTS

I used the example of vomiting and fainting in the worksheet example. The chances of either thing happening are low; however, technically they *could* happen. Reflect on your increasing awareness of how your mind and body, thoughts, and physical symptoms work together during anxiety and panic. What thoughts did you have in response to your physical sensations? For you and your own panic attacks and anxiety, how do your body and mind work together to make things even worse? How did things change when you questioned the likelihood of your thoughts coming true? How can you use awareness and compassion to accept the fact that something bad *might* happen, and move forward anyway?

Interoceptive Exposure

You understand by now that both our thoughts and physical sensations can contribute to our anxiety. You've been exploring the mind-body connection and learning how sensations and thoughts fuel each other. You've also had some practice with exposure therapy, in which you make a plan to intentionally expose yourself to an object or event in the world that causes you to feel anxiety. Today, we'll start to practice a form of exposure that focuses on internal feelings and sensations.

Interoceptive exposure is a strategy in which you intentionally, in a controlled situation, induce the physical sensations associated with anxiety and panic attacks. As in traditional exposure, you gradually learn that your automatic responses to your physical symptom—*I'm having a heart attack! I'm going to pass out!*—aren't really that likely or realistic.

This exercise will deepen your awareness of the precise symptoms you feel in your body and help you accept their occasional presence. The more you do this exercise, the more accustomed you'll become to those sensations. They'll bother you less and less, and your thoughts about them will become more neutral. When you're in a situation that normally triggers a panic attack, you'll notice that your reaction to your increased heart rate or shortness of breath has decreased—and so has your overall anxiety.

Before we start the exercise, it's important to remember that you're not in any panic-inducing or threatening situation right now. You are safe. Keep in mind that as you create the physical symptoms of a panic attack, your thoughts and emotions will likely follow your body. In other words, you may feel increased anxiety, at least at first. While this is a natural response, it can feel quite stressful. You might consider asking someone to sit with you, especially the first time you do this exercise, for emotional support and to help guide you through the deep-breathing exercise.

Now that we've gone over the basics of interoceptive exposure, let's get to it!

WARM-UP

1. Close your eyes and take a deep breath, inhaling and exhaling slowly.

2. Visualize something that causes you anxiety/panic. Be sure to focus on something minor to create mild discomfort rather than full-blown panic attack symptoms.

3. Picture this thing that makes you anxious and imagine that you are there with it right now.

4. Now turn your attention to yourself. What do you notice in your body? Your thoughts? Your emotions? Stay here with these experiences.

5. Open your eyes and allow yourself to return to a calm, relaxed state by taking several slow, deep breaths. Remember that this soothing physical strategy is available to you at any time.

EXERCISE

INTEROCEPTIVE EXPOSURE (PART ONE)

The following are some of the common physical responses to a panic attack. Today, the first time you are taking yourself through this exercise, choose just one or two of them to complete. Start by choosing one, and after you finish it, go on to the next.

Breathing Difficulties

1. Breathe rapidly and shallowly for thirty seconds, mimicking a state of hyperventilation.

2. Scan your body from the top of your head down through your toes. Without being self-critical, observe all of your physical sensations—both big and small.

3. Keep your mindful attention on the sensations in your body, neither judging them nor trying to change them. Be present with them rather than avoiding them.

4. After several minutes, take a few slow, deep breaths to prepare for the next breathing sensation exercise.

Accelerated Heart Rate/Pounding Heart

1. Run in place, up and down the stairs, and/or do jumping jacks for two minutes or until your heart rate increases to the point where you can feel it.

2. Remain standing or sit down, whichever you prefer. Turn your attention to your chest. Without being self-critical, observe all of your physical sensations—both big and small. What do you feel in your chest? How are the effects rippling outward to the rest of your body?

3. Keep your mindful attention on the sensations in your body, neither judging them nor trying to change them. Be present with them rather than avoiding them.

4. After several minutes, take a few slow, deep breaths.

Dizziness

1. Spin in an office chair or stand in a relatively open area and spin. Do this for about one minute or until you feel dizzy, but stop before you fall or get sick.

2. Remain standing or sit down. Your choice.

3. Keep your mindful attention on the sensations in your body, neither judging them nor trying to change them. Be present with them rather than avoiding them.

4. After several minutes, take a few slow, deep breaths.

Head Rush and Vision Disturbances

1. Sit down and bend forward so that your forehead rests on your knees. Remain in this position for 30 to 60 seconds, and then quickly and abruptly stand up.

2. Immediately pick up a book, newspaper, or magazine and attempt to read it.

3. Keep your mindful attention on the sensations in your body, neither judging them nor trying to change them. Be present with them rather than avoiding them.

4. After several minutes, take a few slow, deep breaths.

TURNING INWARD

Describe what it was like for you to stay present with your distressing sensations.

_____

_____

_____

_____

_____

_____

_____

What thoughts did you have during the exercise? Emotions?

_____

_____

_____

_____

_____

_____

_____

_____

DAY 4

INTEROCEPTIVE EXPOSURE (PART TWO)

Congratulations on returning to this place for the second day of the exercise! Your self-commitment and willingness to keep going forward even if something is difficult will ultimately reduce your anxiety and lift its limits from your life.

Part two of this exposure exercise is like part one from yesterday. Today, choose the two bodily sensations that you did not do yesterday. When you've completed them, turn to the following workbook exercise.

EXERCISE

FACING DOWN OBSTACLES

What might get in the way of your continuing to do this exposure exercise?

_____

_____

_____

_____

_____

Give at least three reasons why you will stick with this despite the obstacles you identi-fied. (What will make this exercise worthwhile?)

_____

_____

_____

_____

_____

Peaceful Place Relaxation

Panic attacks and anxiety rev up the mind and body. It's important for your well-being to learn how to relax after a panic attack or after being in an anxiety-provoking situation. Here's an exercise designed to completely relax your body and mind. Practice the exercise after a panic attack or at any time you notice that your body, thoughts, and emotions are caught in an anxious cycle. The body awareness exercises you've learned will help you tune in to when you might benefit from this meditation.

EXERCISE

A SERENE MOUNTAIN MEADOW (15 MINUTES)

1. Set your timer for 15 minutes.

2. Close your eyes and take several slow, deep breaths. Inhale through your nose. Pause. Exhale through your mouth.

3. Imagine that you're standing in the middle of a beautiful mountain meadow. Purple, white, red, and yellow flowers wave gently in the breeze. The sky is a deep blue. Cottony white clouds drift slowly across the sky. Turn slowly and look around you. What else do you see?

4. Continue to breathe slowly and deeply. Smell the mild fragrance of the flowers, allow them to fill your senses.

5. Feel the warmth of the sun on your skin. Turn your face up toward the yellow orb and allow a smile to spread across your face as you enjoy the temperature. You'll feel a warm breeze blow across your skin.

6. You begin to notice gentle sounds, the bubbling sound of a nearby brook. Bees are buzzing in the distance; pay attention to their rhythmic hum. You know that there's nothing to worry about; the bees in this meadow are special. They don't sting. You're free to move about, carefree.

7. You spot a nearby boulder. As you walk toward it, flowers kiss your bare feet, tickling them. A bird soars overhead. You reach the boulder and notice that there is a perfect crevice at the top, just your size. You climb up and wriggle slightly to get comfortable. You fit easily, the boulder cradling you comfortably. It doesn't seem hard at all. It's just right. You place the soles of your feet and the palms of your hands flat on the rock's surface and enjoy the warmth. Once again, you tilt your face to the sun and smile.

8. You sit like that, enjoying the sights, sounds, smells, and physical sensations of this peaceful mountain meadow. Breathe deeply and slowly, reveling in this peaceful place. Your muscles relax, and your whole body seems to melt into your comfortable boulder chair. Enjoy being here.

9. When your timer sounds, look around you. Notice your surroundings. Feel the chair, bed, couch, or floor underneath you. Orient yourself to your present space, and take several slow, deep breaths before getting up.

EXERCISE

A PERSONAL SPACE JUST FOR YOU (15 MINUTES)

Today's relaxation exercise is very similar to yesterday's mountain meadow visualization. The only difference is the setting.

1. Set your timer for 15 minutes.

2. Close your eyes and take several slow, deep breaths. Inhale through your nose. Pause. Exhale through your mouth.

3. Imagine that you're standing inside your home. You recognize the colors of your walls, floors, tables, and other surfaces. Your eyes wander, then settle on a few of your favorite objects and hangings. You smile and enjoy the positive feelings these evoke in you. Now, begin to walk very slowly. What else do you see?

4. Continue to breathe slowly and deeply. Notice the unique smells of your home. You like the way your house smells. It's pleasant and makes you feel happy. What do you smell? Candles? Clean linens?

5. You spot your favorite blanket draped over a chair. You go to it. Rub your hands on it, feeling its softness and texture. Pick it up and wrap it around your shoulders. It feels like a gentle hug, and you feel secure.

6. You have a special room in your house, one you've decorated and furnished just for you. Where is it? Walk to this room now, slowly and deliberately. Feel the floor beneath your bare feet. Hear the subtle sound of your feet walking on the floor. Reach out and run your hand along a wall. What does the texture feel like on your fingertips? What does it sound like?

7. You reach your relaxation room, and you step inside. Take several slow, deep breaths. Look around you. What colors enliven this room? What objects have you placed here? Visualize yourself touching them, picking them up if they're not large and heavy. If you have candles in this room, light them now. Let your gaze fall on your sitting place. Is it a couch? Chair? Pillow? Something else? Go to it now, and settle in. Wriggle your body into a comfortable position. This place is yours, designed just for you, so your body fits perfectly into it. Pull your blanket off your shoulders and drape it over your torso and legs. Revel in this comfort and warmth. Enjoy just being here, in this moment, your whole body soft and relaxed.

8. When your timer sounds, look around you. Notice your surroundings. Feel the chair, bed, couch, or floor underneath you. Orient yourself to your present space, and take several slow, deep breaths before getting up.

EXERCISE

REFLECTION

Create your own peaceful, calming place to use as a relaxation exercise. Use mindfulness to guide you as you craft your image: include elements that stimulate all of your senses. Draw your place, describe it with words, or cut images out of magazines and catalogs to represent this peaceful, anxiety-reducing place.

Homework

As you do these exercises regularly, panic attacks should begin to decrease in frequency and intensity. Tracking your progress along the way will help you see the positive changes and identify what symptoms need extra care and attention. To heighten your awareness of your bodily sensations, thoughts, emotions, and behaviors, consider dedicating a section of your notebook to tracking symptoms. You can assess your symptoms on days when you have a panic attack, or you can do a quick check in daily. These are helpful items to track:

* Date
* Situation that provoked a panic attack or significantly increased my anxiety.
* How did I feel physically? Where did I feel my anxiety?
* What was I thinking about? What was the nature of my thoughts?
* What were my strongest emotions?
* Did I change my plans for the day in any way because of this anxiety or panic?
* What did I do during my panic attack or strong anxiety to keep moving forward?
* What mindfulness techniques and exercises did I use?
* What relaxation exercises or meditations did I use?
* What changes can I notice in my levels of anxiety and panic?
* What is one thing that I can do differently that will keep me moving forward?

TAKEAWAYS

- Panic attacks are the sudden onset of intense physical symptoms of anxiety.

- Panic attacks, like all types of anxiety, affect our thoughts, emotions, physical body, and behaviors.

- The experiences of anxiety attacks and panic attacks are the same, and the terms are often used interchangeably.

- Technically speaking, a panic attack is a major facet of panic disorder, while an anxiety attack isn't part of a disorder but instead is a response that can be triggered by anxiety-provoking situations.

- By using mindful body awareness, you can pull your mind out of the racing thoughts and spiraling emotions you experience during a panic attack. This in turn is calming and reduces feelings of panic and anxiety.

- When you increase your awareness of your physical, emotional, and cognitive symptoms of a panic attack, you also increase your control over your panic attacks and anxiety.

- Mindfulness involves compassion for yourself. Practicing lovingkindness for yourself is an important part of moving past the paralyzing effects of panic attacks.

- Acceptance is vital. When you accept the experience of your panic attacks, you can stop struggling and avoiding and instead use that energy to move forward.

- With mindfulness, including awareness, compassion, and acceptance, you'll take back your life and live with less anxiety and panic.

THE ROAD AHEAD

Long-Term Outlook

You made it! Look how far you've come. Close your eyes, take a few slow, deep breaths, and smile. How does it feel to have completed this book? How is your anxiety these days? My guess is that you likely still have some degree of anxiety. Do you know why this is? It's because you're human. Anxiety can never fully disappear because of the way our brains work. Our fight-or-flight response is a natural part of who we are. It's a part of our biology that we can't change.

Anxiety is part of everyone's life in some shape or form. You'll experience it in varying degrees as you move forward in life. The difference now is that you're no longer paralyzed by anxiety. You know how to reduce its punch and how to break free from its limiting grasp. Welcome to your life without anxiety's restraints.

Keep using the tools in this book. Continue to do the exercises. In order to maintain momentum, do one or two every day. Set aside a dedicated time so it becomes routine, perhaps when you first wake up in the morning or as a relaxing bedtime ritual. You see, mindfulness, awareness, compassion, and acceptance are powerful tools for reducing anxiety in any given moment. When you are deeply familiar with mindfulness exercises, you can call on them to calm you in an anxiety-provoking situation.

Mindfulness and its components are so much more than tools, though. Mindfulness is a way of life. When you live mindfully, you will become less impacted by anxiety. Even when it's there, you'll know instinctively that it's an experience that doesn't define you or dictate your behavior. When you live in such a way that you are in tune with yourself and the moment you're in, you are free to simply be in that given moment.

Keep engaging in the exercises you've learned. You're on the path to breaking free of the shackles of anxiety and moving forward into the quality life you want to live!

Targeting Your Anxiety Challenges

It's impossible for human beings to completely eliminate anxiety, but we can significantly lessen its hold on our lives. Part of managing our anxiety is anticipating when it might show up and coming up with a plan to deal with it when it does. This is a process that involves examining anxiety triggers and what works best to help reduce anxiety.

Ways to catch your anxiety before it strikes:

- **Understand your specific symptoms.** What are your thoughts when your anxiety escalates? In what situations do your symptoms intensify? Lessen?

- **Know what works.** Which strategies are particularly helpful in moments of high anxiety? Perhaps deep breathing or specific mindfulness exercises from this book. Talking to or just being with a support person can help, too.

The next step is to make a plan for how you're going to manage your anxiety when it appears. Creating a written plan is a good idea because it's something concrete that you can hold in your hand and read, which also helps you commit it to memory.

Your plan could look something like this (fill in the blanks):

When I first begin to notice anxiety in my body or mind, I will do these things:

_____

_____

_____

_____

This is how I will use mindfulness to reduce my anxiety in the moment:

_____

_____

_____

If I am feeling particularly unsettled, I will text or call:

_____

_____

_____

_____

This is what I will do every day to maintain a healthy lifestyle and mind-set in order to keep anxiety at bay:

_____

_____

_____

_____

Creating an outlined agenda of how and when to use mindfulness will help you stay in control of your anxiety. Anxiety will occur from time to time, but it doesn't have to dictate your behavior.

Finding What Works for You

Mindfulness is a universal approach that can help everyone lower their anxiety and improve their quality of life. However, since everyone experiences anxiety differently, the strategies for managing your symptoms are individualized and specific to you. To figure out what works best, experiment with the methods outlined in this book until you find the right combination of tactics that both helps reduce your anxiety and suits your life and daily routine. Here are the first steps toward personalizing your anxiety management plan:

- **Make a list.** Start off by writing down a list of the exercises that resonated with you the most. Keeping a running list of strategies that work for you in a bag, drawer, or any other accessible place will help you manage your anxiety if you're feeling too flustered in the moment to remember what to do next. A short, clear list of carefully chosen exercises is better than a long, less focused one.

- **Make a schedule.** Once you have your list, it's important to come up with a schedule of when you're going to practice your exercises on a regular basis. These exercises should become a part of your regular routine—like anything, the more practice, the more you feel the benefits. Doing at least one exercise every day until it becomes a habit is the best way to develop an empowering routine that, ultimately, will transform both your relationship to anxiety and your life.

Additionally, these tips can help you create and customize a sustainable mindfulness maintenance program:

- **Choose a time of day to practice mindfulness.** Having a regular schedule helps you stick to it.

- **Choose a setting where you'll have a comfortable place to sit or lie down.** Fill the space with furniture, decorations, and objects that bring you happiness.

- **Make your practice a ritual.** Have tea or another soothing, nonalcoholic, noncaffeinated beverage. Put on soothing, meditative music or keep the room silent, whichever you prefer. Maybe light a candle or use an essential oil diffuser.

- **Don't restrict yourself.** If you have a meeting or any other kind of obligation that cuts into the middle of your regular mindfulness time, let yourself make the necessary adjustments without feeling anxious about it. Regular practice encourages you to develop the mindfulness habit and will go a long way in reducing anxiety, but that doesn't mean that you have to be rigid.

- **Find ways to enrich and enjoy your practice.** Think of it as a pleasurable time, rather than a burden or chore. In our frenetic, overscheduled lives, taking a break for quiet and reflection can be a real treat! Remember your reason for practicing mindfulness: to live a quality life, free from anxiety's control. Knowing your purpose will help you stay motivated to continue regular, consistent practice.

Finding Support

Throughout these exercises, you've infinitely increased opportunities for positive change in your life. You've gained the knowledge and skills to actively reduce your anxiety and start living in the moment. However, these lessons also bring about new challenges and frustrations. When you've developed a stable mindfulness routine, it's not uncommon to experience flares of anxiety from time to time. These flares are temporary, but they don't always *feel* temporary when they happen. It's important to remain aware that they will pass, and to have a support system of people you can count on and trust when anxiety strikes.

Support can take many forms: friendships, therapists, organizations, and support groups. Find support both online and in the real world you live in. Not all support systems are right for everyone. Some people might benefit from regular sessions with a therapist, whereas others do better in group settings.

Since it can be overwhelming to begin the search for the right kind of anxiety support system, I've compiled this brief list of ideas to get you started:

THERAPY WITH A MENTAL HEALTH PROFESSIONAL

- Ask your primary physician for recommendations.

- Use therapist-finder features on PsychologyToday.com or GoodTherapy.org. They will help you filter therapists based on your location and insurance plan.

- Libraries and community centers often display pamphlets, cards, and brochures from local therapists and mental health organizations.

- If you can't find a suitable therapist in your area, consider virtual therapy. There are more and more online resources for video-based therapy. Talkspace.com and betterhelp.com are two reputable places to start your search.

SUPPORT GROUPS

- AnxietyCentral offers multiple forums for different anxiety challenges and disorders: www.anxiety-central.com.

- AnxietyCommunity hosts numerous forums for anxiety and other mental health topics: www.anxietycommunity.com.

- Social Anxiety Support is an archive of resources and articles on how to manage social anxiety: www.socialanxietysupport.com.

- The Anxiety and Depression Association of America (ADAA) has online support groups and a support group finder so you can see what anxiety support groups are in your area: www.adaa.org/supportgoups.

- The National Alliance on Mental Illness (NAMI) offers community-based general support groups for people experiencing any mental health challenge, including anxiety. Visit www.nami.org to find an affiliate near you.

- MeetUp.com is a resource for finding local groups and events. You can search for anxiety support groups, mindfulness groups, and more.

- Check with local mental health and other health care professionals. They have the most up-to-date information on specific support groups.

ONLINE MINDFULNESS COURSES

There is a wide range of virtual mindfulness courses for anyone wanting to explore mindfulness on a deeper level:

- Sounds True: www.soundstrue.com/store

- Online Courses: www.onlinecollegecourses.com/2012/11/25/9 -great-mindfulness-courses-you-can-take-online

- Palouse Mindfulness: https://palousemindfulness.com

Support groups and online forums can help you gain another perspective on your anxiety. Similar to individualized therapy, they give you the opportunity to share your experiences, listen to others, and give and receive feedback.

You're now on the road to embracing a mindful way of life. Keep your momentum going, and keep practicing, so you can be fully present for the rich, rewarding life you want to live!

MORE RESOURCES

These websites, books, hotlines, and articles are extensive resources to help you learn more about anxiety and mindfulness:

Books

Arriving at Your Own Door: 108 Lessons in Mindfulness by Jon Kabat-Zinn

Break Free: Acceptance and Commitment Therapy in 3 Steps—A Workbook for Overcoming Self-Doubt and Embracing Life by Tanya J. Peterson

Calm: Calm the Mind, Change the World by Michael Acton Smith

Complete Book of Mindful Living: Awareness and Meditation Practices for Living in the Present Moment by Robert Butera and Erin Byron

Declutter Your Mind: How to Stop Worrying, Relieve Anxiety, and Eliminate Negative Thinking by S.J. Scott and Barrie Davenport

Mindfulness for Beginners: Reclaiming the Present Moment—and Your Life by Jon Kabat-Zinn

Articles

3 Quick Mindfulness Practices to Overcome Worry, Anxiety, and Panic by Jodie Gien: www.everyday-mindfulness.org/3-quick-mindfulness-practices-to-overcome -worry-anxiety-and-panic

10 Mindful Attitudes that Decrease Anxiety by Bob Stahl: www.mindful.org/10-mindful-attitudes-decrease-anxiety

Mindfulness-Based Stress Reduction (MBSR) for Anxiety by Tanya J. Peterson:
www.healthyplace.com/blogs/anxiety-schmanxiety/2017/10/mindfulness-based
-stress-reduction-mbsr-for-anxiety-treatment

Using Mindfulness for Anxiety: Here's How by Tanya J. Peterson: www.healthyplace.com
/self-help/anxiety/using-mindfulness-for-anxiety-here-s-how

Using Mindfulness to Treat Anxiety disorders by George Hofmann: www.psychcentral
.com/blog/archives/2013/01/28/using-mindfulness-to-treat-anxiety-disorders

What is Mindfulness? UC Berkeley's The Greater Good Magazine: greatergood.berkeley
.edu/mindfulness/definition

Websites

These reputable sites offer reliable anxiety information and support:

- Anxiety and Depression Association of America (ADAA): www.adaa.org
- Anxiety Centre: www.anxietycentre.com
- Anxiety Coach: www.anxietycoach.com
- Calm Clinic: www.calmclinic.com
- HealthyPlace: www.healthyplace.com
- Psych Central: www.psychcentral.com

Excellent, reliable mindfulness websites include:

- The Free Mindfulness Project: www.freemindfulness.org
- Mindful: www.mindful.org
- Mindfulnet: The Mindfulness Information Website: www.mindfulnet.org
- Pocket Mindfulness: www.pocketmindfulness.com

Hotlines

The Anxiety Hotline Number article on Mental Health Help provides useful information about anxiety and how to use hotline numbers: www.mentalhelp.net/articles /anxiety-hotline. The article also provides the following hotline numbers:

National Alliance on Mental Illness (NAMI): call 1-800-950-NAMI (6264) Monday-Friday 10 a.m. to 6 p.m. Eastern time or visit www.nami.org for more information.

National Suicide Prevention Lifeline: call 1-800-273-TALK (8255) or visit www.suicidepreventionlifeline.org for an online chat service.

Substance Abuse and Mental Health Services Administration (SAMHSA): call 1-800-662-HELP (4375) or visit www.samhsa.gov/find-help/national-helpline for more information.

Boys Town National Hotline: Helps teens, but parents can call as well; call 1-800-448-3000 or visit www.boystown.org/hotline/Pages for e-mail, text, and online chat services.

Teen Line: call 1-310-855-HOPE (4673) or 1-800-TLC-TEEN (852-8336), text "TEEN" to 839863 from 6 p.m. to 9 p.m. Pacific time, or visit teenlineonline.org for e-mail and message board options.

Help Finding a Therapist: 1-800-THERAPIST (843-7274)

Panic Disorder Information Hotline: 1-800-64-PANIC (647-2642)

REFERENCES

Altman, Donald. *The Mindfulness Toolbox: 50 Practical Tips, Tools, and Handouts for Anxiety, Depression, Stress, and Pain.* Eau Claire, WI: Pesi Publishing and Media, 2014.

American Psychiatric Association. *Diagnostic and Statistical Manual of Mental Disorders, Fifth Edition (DSM-5).* Arlington, VA: American Psychological Association, 2013.

Antony, Martin M. and Karen Rowa. *Social Anxiety Disorder.* Cambridge: Hogrefe and Huber Publishers, 2008.

Berenbaum, Howard, Keith Bredemeier, and Renee J. Thompson. "Intolerance of Uncertainty: Exploring its Dimensionality and Associations with Need for Cognitive Closure, Psychopathology, and Personality." *Journal of Anxiety Disorders* 22 (2008): 117–125. pages.wustl.edu/emotionlab/berenbaum-bredemeier-thompson-2008

Bourne, Edmund J. *The Anxiety and Phobia Workbook, Fifth Edition.* Oakland: New Harbinger Publications, 2010.

Boyes, Alice. "Avoidance Coping: Avoidance Coping Plays an Important Role in Common Psychological Problems." Psychology Today. May 5, 2013. www.psychologytoday.com/blog/in-practice/201305/avoidance-coping

Butera, Robert and Erin Byron. *Complete Book of Mindful Living: Awareness and Meditation Practices for Living in the Present Moment.* Woodbury, MN: Llewellyn

Dahlgren, Kate. "That's a Problem for Future Homer: Avoidance Learning." Emotion on the Brain: The Neuroscience of Emotion: From Reaction to Regulation, Tufts University. October 24, 2014. Accessed December 10, 2017. sites.tufts.edu/emotiononthebrain/2014/10/24/thats-a-problem-for-future-homer-avoidance-learning

Daitch, Carolyn. *Anxiety Disorders: The Go-To Guide for Clients and Therapists.* New York: Norton, 2011.

"Facts and Statistics." Anxiety and Depression Association of America, ADAA. Accessed November 16, 2017. adaa.org/about-adaa/press-room/facts-statistics

Flaxman, Greg, and Lisa Flook. "Brief Summary of Mindfulness Research." Accessed November 17, 2017. www.marc.ucla.edu/workfiles/pdfs/MARC-mindfulness -research-summary.pdf

Forsyth, John and Georg Eifert. *The Mindfulness and Acceptance Workbook for Anxiety: A Guide to Breaking Free from Anxiety, Phobias, and Worry Using Acceptance and Commitment Therapy.* Oakland: New Harbinger, 2007.

Horsyt, Britta K., James Carmody, Mark Vangel, Christina Congleton, Sita M. Yerramsetti, Tim Gard, and Sara W. Lazar. "Mindfulness Practice Leads to Increases in Regional Brain Gray Matter Density." *Psychiatry Research: Neuroimaging* 191, no. 1 (January 30, 2011): 36–43. doi:10.1016/j.pscychresns.2010.08.006.

Kabat-Zinn, Jon. *Coming to Our Senses: Healing Ourselves and The World Through Mindfulness.* New York: Hachette Books, 2005.

Kabat-Zinn, Jon. *Mindfulness for Beginners: Reclaiming the Present Moment—and Your Life.* Boulder, CO: Sounds True, 2016.

Leahy, Robert L. "'But What if I'm THE ONE?' How Intolerance of Uncertainty Makes You Anxious." *Psychology Today.* May 14, 2008. Accessed December 8, 2017. www.psychologytoday.com/blog/anxiety-files/200805/what-if-im-the-one-how -intolerance-uncertainty-makes-you-anxious.

Lejeune, Chad. *The Worry Trap: How to Free Yourself from Worry & Anxiety Using Acceptance & Commitment Therapy.* Oakland, CA: New Harbinger Publications, 2007.

Lee, Kiyoe, Yumiko Noda, Yumi Nakano, Sei Ogawa, Yoshihiro Kinoshita, Tadashi Funayama, and Toshiaki A. Furukawa. "Interoceptive Hypersensitivity and Interoceptive Exposure in Patients with Panic Disorder: Specificity and Effectiveness." *BMC Psychiatry* 6, no. 32. (August 2006). doi:10.1186/1471-244X-6-32.

Peterson, Tanya J. "Anxiety: It's in Your Head (Your Brain!)." Anxiety-Schmanxiety Blog, HealthyPlace. February 20, 2014. Retrieved December 1, 2017. www.healthyplace. com/blogs/anxiety-schmanxiety/2014/02/anxiety-its-in-your-head-your-brain.

Peterson, Tanya J. *Break Free: Acceptance and Commitment Therapy in 3 Steps— A Workbook for Overcoming Self-Doubt and Embracing Life.* Berkeley, CA: Althea Press, 2016.

Peterson, Tanya J. *My Life in a Nutshell: A Novel.* Portland: Inkwater Press, 2014.

Richards, Thomas A. "Basic Facts about Panic Attacks." The Anxiety Network. Accessed December 28, 2017. www.anxietynetwork.com/content/basic-facts-panic-attacks.

Trungpa, Chöryam. *Mindfulness in Action: Making Friends with Yourself through Meditation and Everyday Awareness.* edited by Carolyn Rose Gimian. Boulder, CO: Shambhala, 2016.

INDEX

ABOUT THE AUTHOR

Tanya J. Peterson, MS, NCC, earned her master's degree in counseling from South Dakota State University and holds credentials as a national certified counselor. She writes extensively for the mental health website HealthyPlace. com, including her weekly Anxiety-Schmanxiety column. She is a prolific writer of online and print articles on mental health and is a frequent speaker and radio show guest. Additionally, she is the author of five critically acclaimed, award-winning novels that address mental health themes. She created a curriculum about toxic relationships based on her middle-grade/YA novel *Losing Elizabeth;* she takes both to schools and community programs. She also writes self-help books that people can use to help themselves create quality lives. Visit TanyaJPeterson.com to learn more about Tanya and to connect with her.

CPSIA information can be obtained
at www.ICGtesting.com
Printed in the USA
JSHW021846161019
1931JS00001B/1